Advanced Academic Writing 482

An Illustrated Program

Volume Two

OCTOBER 2009

Student Manual

Michael Clay Thompson

Royal Fireworks Press
Unionville, New York

Roble 1

Barney Roble

Ms. DeMeener

English Honors

25 April 2008

The Noble Character of Alexander

The literature about Alexander the Great is ex

Writers ancient and modern have probed the availa

of his life in search of the factors that enable

to accomplish seemingly impossible feats of mili

One potential cause of his extraordinary succes

nobility and magnanimity of his character. S

about Alexander's respect for local cultures a

absorbed de

Works Cited   Roble 4

Cartledge, Paul. *Alexander the Great.* New York: Overlook,
        2004.

Cummings, Lewis V. *Alexander the Great.* New York: Grove,
        1968.

Fox, Robin Lane

Royal Fireworks Press
First Avenue, PO Box 399
Unionville, NY 10988-0399
(845) 726-4444
FAX: (845) 726-3824
email: mail@rfwp.com
website: rfwp.com
ISBN:
Student Book: 978-0-88092-676-8
Teacher Book: 978-0-88092-677-5

Printed and bound in the United States of America using vegetable-
based inks on acid-free recycled paper and environmentally-friendly
cover coatings by the Royal Fireworks Printing Co. of Unionville, New York.

Design and text by Michael Clay Thompson

Table of Contents

Odomini 1

Ann Odomini

Ms. Givings

English Honors

14 February 2008

Two Views of Ethnocentrism

Anthropologists have studied hundreds of cultures in search of what have been called *cultural universals*, and they have identified dozens of traits and patterns that exist in every known society. These include such traits as marriage, language, trade, etiquette, property, weapons, toys, beliefs, myths, and cooking. Not all anthropologists, however, agree on all traits, and it is the points of disagreement that are _____ the areas where research

4

Mort Ishun

Ms. Ereecord

English II

14 May 2009

The Structure of *Romeo and Juliet*'s Prologue

Because the meaning of the words so capture our attention, **S/V**

it is easy to read the prologue to William Shakespeare's *Romeo*

and Juliet about "Two households, both alike in dignity, / In

fair Verona, where we lay our scene" (1-2) without realizing

that the prologue is an English sonnet: a fourteen-line poem,

in iambic pentameter, containing three quatrains and a couplet.

The sonnet's first quatrain is a single sentence that

presents the families, the scene of Verona and the blood feud

that makes "civil hands unclean" (4), but the second quattrain **SP**

--which is also a single sentence--introduces the "star-crossed

lovers" who are the main figures of the play:

> From forth the fatal loins of these two foes
> A pair of star-crossed lovers take their life;
> Whose misadventured piteous overthrows
> Do with their death bury their parents' strife. (5-8)

The rhyme scheme adheres strictly to the requirements of

a sonnet, with the first quatrain's dignity-scene-mutiny-unclean

establishing the abab, and the second quatrain's foes-life-

overthrows-strife forming the cdcd. The creative dignity-

mutiny rhyme is characteristic of Shakespeare's play with

In this paper the numbers in the parentheticals refer to the line numbers of the poem.

Works Cited

Crackcorn, James. *I Don't Care: How to Hear Poetry for the First Time.* New York: Paladin, 2007.

Effant, Elle. *Julio and Romiet.* Chicago: Trove, 2001.

Shakespeare, William. Romeo and Juliet. London: Admiralty, **ital**
2007.

Zeno, Eevul. "More than Rhyme: An Examination of Poetic Devices within the Lines of Shakespeare's Plays." *The Manchester Poetry Review.* 46 (2003): 173-197.

1. YOUR WRITING

First, let us talk about you. The purpose of this book is not simply to praise writing; it is to make a writer of you. Every word of this book is really about you. The very design of this book is based on what I assume about you, so you need to know what my assumptions about you are:

I think you want a book that assumes your maturity. You do not want a book that talks down to you. You want a serious, strong book that teaches you advanced things in an advanced way. You are ready for that and prefer it.

I think you are smart. I think that I can say something one time, in as few words as possible, and you will click into comprehension. You do not want me to waste your time, to say things five ways, or repeat them five times. I think we can go fast. I can write this book in a tight way, trusting your intensity and concentration. I think you would rather concentrate than be distracted.

I think you do not need constantly to be entertained. You do not need an approach that tries to make academic writing *seem* interesting; it *is* interesting, and you know that without my saying it. You think it is fun to do advanced work. You want to work hard and to be intense about something so important. You do not need me to get you excited about academic writing; you already are.

I think you want to learn important knowledge, permanently. You do not want activities about minor facts that you will forget when the unit ends. You want major knowledge, and work that will make it stick. You want to be educated.

I think you want challenge, and that you know it is more fun to work hard on something good than to be bored with something that is too easy or too trivial.

I think you want the truth. It might, for example, be relaxing to ignore the fact that many of your future teachers and professors are going to grade your writing severely—but they are, and it is better for you to face it now and get ready, than to avoid it now and be caught unprepared. You do not want to realize—too late—that the admonitions you received earlier were true. You want to be prepared.

I think you will believe me. I think I can tell you that the academic world demands a particular detail (or dozens of them) to be thus, and you will believe me. I think you will believe me if I tell you that yes, this is a challenge to learn, and it means hard work, but the more you learn about writing, the more you will love writing—not just casual writing which is fun too, but excellent academic writing.

I think you and I will be on the same page.

TWO POSSIBLE FUTURES

You have a future as a writer; there is no doubt about that. The question is, what future? Let us assume—and this is a safe assumption—that you will take challenging academic courses in high school and then pursue a college or university degree. For four years most of your college professors will base part (sometimes all) of your semester grades on the papers you write—formal papers, typed on a computer word processor, written in correct academic English, and prepared according to the strict standards of a national format such as the MLA (Modern Language Association) method. You may even take courses in which formal papers are due every week (I had two such courses at the same time in one of my college semesters). You may have semesters at college where you have papers due in *all* of your courses.

There are two possible futures—good and bad—in which you might find yourself, each one the result of decisions that you make now. The bad future is that you will dread writing assignments, that every time a formal paper is due, you will be filled with anxiety and uncertain about how to write such a paper. You will not know correct grammar and punctuation. You will feel overwhelmed by the demands of the format (such as the MLA method). You will have to suffer the stress, extra work, and expense of paying someone to type your paper. You will regard writing papers as the worst part of your college experience. You will hope—in self-delusion—that you will be done with such writing once you are out of college (You will be in for a shock).

The good future is that when you receive your formal writing assignments, you will understand the English standards, will appreciate the clarity and simplicity of the (often MLA) format, and will be glad that you type well so that you can be certain the paper is typed the way the professor expects it. You will have enough confidence about your standard English that you can enjoy the knowledge and ideas of the topic and experience research as a deep learning opportunity. You will be grateful that you have written so many academic papers because the experience has prepared you for major careers for which you would otherwise not have been qualified.

The purpose of *Advanced Academic Writing*, Volume Two, is to prepare you for the second future, so that you can enjoy academic writing and thrive in the academic environment. This book is Volume Two in a series of three that will prepare you to write the advanced academic papers you will have to submit in honors high school and college courses. Volume Two incorporates but goes beyond the introductory instruction of Volume One. This means that in the assignments of this book, you will be expected to exhibit—and will be held responsible for—the four elements of English, essay form, MLA format, and intellectual content that were introduced in Volume One.

Volume One is basic; it explains the standards of academic writing, the elements of essay structure, and the first principles of an MLA research paper. It introduces ten standard proofreader's marks used by teachers, professors, and editors, and it reviews the rules of punctuation, usage, and grammar that must be followed in a formal paper. Volume One presents forty actual research paper comments that I have made and archived on student papers during a period of decades; these comments emphasize common errors that students are likely to make. To all of this knowledge, we must now add new details and new elements.

In Volume Two you will extend your competence on every front. To maintain what you have learned in Volume One, you will find all of the elements you already studied, but now you will encounter a new array of requirements. You will have more elaborate MLA format rules to follow, more competent essay continuity to forge, more proofreader's marks to decipher, and forty more actual research paper comments to absorb.

I hope that you did study Volume One and are ready to build on that foundation. If not, then you will need to do some extra study—there is nothing wrong with that—to get in sync with this book. I do not want you to have to juggle two books back and forth, so I am including, once again, Volume One's summaries of the punctuation, usage, and grammar rules expected in a formal paper, as well as the forty actual research paper comments from Volume One—all of those reappear in this book, so that you can review them easily.

2. VOLUME ONE AND MORE

In *Advanced Academic Writing* Volume One we studied four basic elements of advanced academic writing: standard English, correct format (MLA is what we use), essay structure, and a meaningful thesis. Here are summaries of some of the key points in Volume One, with additional information that builds on that foundation.

THE LOGIC OF THE ESSAY

A scholarly essay is a three-part logical development of one idea, called the *thesis*. The three parts are the **introduction**, the **body**, and the **conclusion**. An essay can be as short as five paragraphs, but it can also be much longer. An academic essay must adhere to the standards of correct English grammar and punctuation. Within the essay the paragraphs must follow a logical sequence, and each paragraph must be organized, with sentences only about its topic. Special linking words must connect the paragraphs to one another. The conclusion must collect the facts and ideas of the body and extract their meaning. The complete structure creates a tight logic system for presenting ideas.

Look carefully at the essay structure on the facing page. It is like a telescope, a high-precision instrument with clear lenses that bring everything to a pinpoint focus. The conclusion is the eye-piece, where all of the information converges to a point.

In an excellent academic essay, not one idea is out of sequence, and not one piece is unnecessary. Every detail supports the crisp thesis, which is first introduced, then explained in a logical sequence, and then brought to a conclusion in a way that gathers all of the parts together to form the main point of the paper.

Jones 5

Works Cited

Adamsand, Molly Cules. *Mashed Potatoes and Gravity*. Atlanta: Vista, 2004.

Poole, Claire. *The Moon Keeps Its Distance*. Philadelphia: Alantis UP, 2001.

Mudd, Del. *Gravitation Is Attractive*. New York: Blogwin, 2007.

Watson, I-Wanchu. *A Lexi-Gram Bell*. Boston: U of Boston P, 1996.

The strategy of the essay is simplicity. Everything is focused on one point.

$t?$ **INTRODUCTION**
Introduce Thesis

t^1 **BODY**
Develop Thesis

a
b
c
d

t^2 **BODY**
Develop Thesis

a
b
c
d

t^3 **BODY**
Develop Thesis

a
b
c
d

$t!$ **CONCLUSION**
Conclude Thesis

1

2

3

STANDARD PROOFREADER'S MARKS

Even correction can be correct. Certain proofreading marks are standard throughout the publishing and academic worlds. You can learn these standard marks now, and see them employed by teachers, professors, and editors in your future. In Volume One we studied ten standard proofreader's marks. We will now increase the list to twenty.

1.	Delete	I have my very own example.
2.	Insert period	Clouds approached⊙ It rained.
3.	Insert comma	He was strict, stern⌄and serious.
4.	Insert space	Alexander reacted⌄quickly. #
5.	Close up	Suddenly, the bat‿tle began.
6.	Start new paragraph	It ended. ¶ The next day we departed.
7.	Spell out or spelling error	It was the ④th time that week. (sp)
8.	Transpose (switch)	It began to (suddenly rain) (tr)
9.	Awkward wording	It went then higher as a thing gradual. (awk)
10.	Subject/verb disagreement	The reason for the errors (are) this. s/v
11.	Insert apostrophe	We saw the brigades slow advance.
12.	Lower case	Dickens was a student of History. (lc)
13.	Italics	The word <u>chicken</u> sounds funny. (ital)
14.	Capitalize	The english defeated the armada. (cap)
15.	Insert hyphen	They fired off a one⌄gun salute. =/
16.	Insert text	It was⌄highest mountain. /the
17.	Leave unchanged	The ~~freezing~~ blue day broke slowly. (STET)
18.	Sentence fragment	<u>As we began.</u> The door opened. frag
19.	Run-on sentence	Monet painted steadily⌄and the work grew. R-O
20.	Pronoun problem	Everyone lost <u>their</u> sense of humor. pron

Your teachers, professors, and editors will use these proofreader's marks with a degree of flexibility. For example, some of them are circled, but that is not a fixed rule. The marks are usually circled but mean the same thing if not circled.

A mark within the line may be accompanied by a mark in the margin, such as in number 13 when we underline the word *chicken* and then put *ital* out in the margin, or in number 20 when we underline the offensive pronoun and then put *pron* in the margin.

The mark *ital* means italics. In the past when typewriters could not make *true italics*, we used underlining to indicate italics. Particularly in the Courier type font, underlining looked better than italics. Today, computers can create italics in all fonts, and the Modern Language Association has discontinued underlining; we now use true italics for titles of books, journals, and newspapers, ships, foreign words, as well as for words as such.

The word *stet* is Latin, meaning "Let it stand." It means that the editor has changed his or her mind (or disagrees with a prior proofreader) and wants a previous correction mark to be ignored. *Stet* is sometimes in all-caps, sometimes not.

In addition to the marks at left, you may see *ww*, wrong word; *ref*, unclear pronoun reference; or *mm*, misplaced modifier.

Thyme 1

Mari Thyme

Mr. Oshundiep

Biology 1H

7 October 2009

　　　　　　The Unique Nature of Cephalopod Intelligence

　　The cephalopods, which include the octopi and the squid (the plural of *squid* is either *squid* or *squids*), are the most intelligent invertebrates. They have large brians and solve (sp) problems in ways that involve the articulate tentacles that (ital) emerge from their heads. In his Scientific Biology article "The Cephalopods Are Fully Armed," Kingston University marine biologist Mark Phathum explains that "the cephalopoda have more complex nervous systems than gastropods do and exhibit more awareness of their environment" (Phathum 115-116). Biologist Minny Leegs agrees, adding that:

　　　Cephalopod intelligence may be a function of their multiple tentacles, the use and coordination of which requires substantial neural processing. Without their nervous complex system, cephalopods could not (tr) exist as we know them. (Leegs 217)

Works Cited

Leegs, Minny. *The Soft-Headed Squid*. Chi[...]
　　Lake Shore UP, 2002.

Phathum, Mark. "The Cephalopods Are Full A[...]
　　Biology 2 (2006): 42-57.

MLA FORMAT

The MLA (Modern Language Association) research paper method is the most widely adopted standard in the world, used in more high schools, colleges, and universities than any other. MLA is more standard in literary and humanities papers than in the sciences, but it is also used in those areas and is the simplest format to use when you are first learning. It has achieved this acceptance because of this clarity and simplicity. Our papers will be prepared on a computer word processor (advanced papers are not handwritten), using the MLA format exclusively, and without deviation from its standards. For complete details, see the *MLA Handbook*, but here are some fundamental elements:

1. A **one-inch margin** on all four sides of the paper.
2. The entire paper is **double-spaced**, including long quotations.
3. The text is **ragged right**, not justified.
4. One-half inch from the top of every page is a **header** with the student's name followed by the page number. There is no comma after the name.
5. There is **no separate title page**; the title information appears at the top of page one; this includes the student's name, the teacher's name, the name of the course, and the date; all of this is flush left. This is followed by the title of the paper, exactly centered.
6. The **title should not be underlined**, put in quotations, or in all-capital letters. If a book title that should be in italics is in the paper's title, then italicize only the book title.
7. Instead of footnotes, MLA documents quotations or other borrowings with **parenthetical documentation**, consisting of the author's name and the page number enclosed in parentheses, like this: (Thompson 12). The author's name in any parenthetical must appear in the alphabetical list of authors that appears on the Works Cited page. Subsequent quotations from an author may include page number only.
8. **Long quotations** of four lines or more are **indented ten spaces**. The parenthetical for a long quote comes after the period, but for a short quote it comes before.
9. Instead of a Bibliography page at the end of the paper, MLA uses a **Works Cited** page. On the Works Cited page, authors cited are listed alphabetically. Names in parentheticals appear in this list. Publishers in the listings are abbreviated; Random House is simply Random, Harvard University Press is Harvard UP. We will review the Works Cited instructions in the first assignment.
10. **Do not put the paper in a separate cardboard or plastic cover**. Do not punch holes in the paper. Staple the paper in the top left corner.

Stottel 1

Ari Stottel

Ms. Takenthot

World History

22 October 2009

Curious Questions in Plato's *Dialogues*

Plato's *Dialogues* present Socrates as a gadfly philosopher, beseiging weary Athenians with questions that lead them, finally, to the realization that they know less than they thought they knew. Was Socrates merely using questions to make others agree with him, or did Socrates himself think that the ultimate answers were unknown? Was Socrates's famous paradox, "I only know that I know nothing" (Plato 94), sincere?

In *The Real Question about Socrates*, Dan Delyfe, professor of philosophy at Addle University, says that Socrates:

. . . did not use his dialogues with other Athenians to steer them into agreement with himself, but to unearth the contradictions and biases that lurked in their half-formed ideas. (Delyfe 73)

Delyfe argues that Socrates's sincerity is "evident from his lack of any articulated philosophical ideas" (94) and from the fact that he never took "measures to record his thought or make it permanent" (173).

Ellah Mentarry, professor of ancient history at Haryard University, disagrees, noting that the "orthodox view of Socratic thought is more persuasive" (Mentarry 428). She explains: "In Socrates's Athens there were three leading

---

The MLA format is designed to be ultra-clear and easy to read.

Stottel 4

Works Cited

Azance, Wren. *The False Deconstruction of Truth*. Los Angeles: Chaparral UP, 2009.

Dissie, Theo. "Was Socrates an Evil Genius?" *The Journal of Ethical Inquiry* 7 (2003): 256-74.

Delyfe, Dan. *The Real Question about Socrates*. New York: U of Addle P, 2004.

Mentarry, Ellah. *Out of the Question*. Chicago: Haryard UP, 2001.

Plato. *Dialogues*. Boston: Stork, 2004.

Sizzum, Sol I. Introduction. *Reason to Doubt*. By Noah Count. New York: Rumple, 1989. vi-xvi.

PUNCTUATION

In Volume One we reviewed punctuation standards. Here are those rules again, so that you can have them for easy reference. This time I will put the rules on the left page and special comments about some of them on the right page. Many of these same ideas will also necessarily appear again in the list of actual research paper comments. Pay special attention to those marked with a blue pencil: ✎ .

comma: (,)

    after introductory participial phrases: `Grabbing the rope, Bo blinked.`

    after introductory interjections: `No, I want no geese present.`

    after informal salutations: `Dear Absalom, you are a rustler.`

    after long introductory prepositional phrases:
        `After a very bad giggle, Elenor randomly glanced.`

✎   **after multiple introductory prepositional phrases:**
        `At the back of the boat at the dock, Hiram reflected.`

✎   **after introductory dependent clauses (D,I):** `As he left, we began again.`

    after the day and year: On `March 12, 2008, Marcus meandered.`

    after the city and state: `Abilene, Texas, was the wrong place to be.`

    around nonessential (nonrestrictive) clauses:
        `Daryl Darrel, who is my uncle, decided to demur.`

    around nonessential participial phrases:
        `Lou, noticing nothing, nudged the petunia.`

✎   **around most appositives:** `Mose Osaur, the Nobel Prize winner, replied.`

    around nouns of direct address: `Yes, Luanne, the loam looks lighter.`

    around parenthetical expressions: `Two tons, enough for anyone, arrived.`

✎   **before coordinating conjunctions in I,ccI compound sentences:**
        `Madeline made models, and Hedda had ham.`

✎   **between all items in a list:** `Eggbert ate eggs, eggs, eggs, eggs, and eggs.`

✎   **between *coordinate* adjectives preceding a noun:** `Find a short, green stalk.`

    between contrasts introduced by *not*: `I want boats, not goats.`

    between name and degree or title: `Jeffers Thomason, Ph.D.`

    inside closing quotation marks: `"Shut up," he explained.`

✎   **NOT between *cumulative* adjectives preceding a noun:** `Get five blue ones.`

    NOT after a short prepositional phrase: `For you I found four yew.`

    NOT between compound subjects/predicates: `Sleepy and Dopey were mopey.`

    NOT between subject and verb: Wrong: `July, is named for Julius Caesar.`

Commas in D,I and I,ccI Clause Structures

Every sentence you write has one or more clauses, so you must understand the clause punctuation rules. When a **complex sentence** has the dependent clause before the independent clause, we put a comma after that introductory dependent clause. If we let **D** stand for dependent clause, **I** stand for independent clause, and **cc** stand for coordinating conjunction, we can express the clause punctuation rules in shorthand. A complex sentence beginning with a dependent clause would be **D,I**. Examples of correct **D,I** sentences:

> When the novel was finished, Hemingway left for Idaho.

> If Alexander had not attacked immediately, Darius might have won the battle.

> Because x + 3 = 7, we know that x = 4.

If a **compound sentence** has a coordinating conjunction joining the two independent clauses, we put a comma before the conjunction to keep the two clauses apart. We can express the rule as **I,ccI**. Examples of correct **I,ccI** sentences:

> Churchill reassured the nation, but the bombs continued to fall.

> The poem must have fourteen lines, or it is not a sonnet.

> The tropical water was warm, and schools of fish swarmed over the reef.

Commas after Introductory Participial Phrases

A participle is a verb that is acting as an adjective. If we say that *the running man escaped*, the adjective *running* is a participle; it is made out of a verb, but in this sentence it is an adjective modifying the noun *man*. One of the most important of all grammar structures is the introductory participial phrase, as in ***Walking his dog**, Randolf headed toward the park*. In this sentence the subject is *Randolf*, and the verb is *headed*. The sentence begins with an introductory participial phrase, *walking his dog*, which modifies *Randolf*. There are two important rules here. One is that the **introductory participial phrase must modify the subject**, or else you might have a ridiculous **misplaced modifier** such as *Slurping ice cream, the tree shaded Robert's head*. In this sentence the phrase was intended to modify *Robert*, but it always modifies the subject, so we have a tree that is slurping ice cream. The second rule is that **the introductory participial phrase must be set off by a comma**. Here are some correct examples; notice how the participial phrase always modifies the subject of the sentence:

> Counting the change, Maria wondered what she could buy.

> Descending in the darkness, Daniel stepped carefully over the ice.

> Eating the frog quickly, the heron stared across the marsh.

semicolon: (;)

✎ **between independent clauses if no coordinating conjunction: I;I**
> The time is out of joint; I must depart immediately.

between items in a list if the items themselves contain commas:
> Get me grits; green, growing grass; and grippers.

between independent clauses joined by *however*, etc.
> I literally laughed; however, you laterally loafed.

colon: (:)

before a list that is not a compound direct object or subject complement:
> Bring this list: apples, paddles, dappled plaids.

before a long formal statement: To my extinguished friends:

✎ **before a long quotation, as in a research paper.**

between hours and minutes in time: 6:15

between Bible chapter and verse: John 1:23

after formal salutations: Dear Mr. Applegate:

✎ **between titles and subtitles:** *Walt Whitman: Poet of America*

italics: (*italics*) (In the past, underline was the same thing.)

✎ **title of a book:** *A Tale of Two Cities*

✎ **title of a magazine:** *Life*

title of a work of art: *Mona Lisa*

title of a train or airplane: *Spirit of St. Louis*

✎ **words, letters, and numbers as such:** the word *blubber*, the letter *a*, and the number *5*

foreign language words: *dejà vu*

quotation marks: (" ")

around a direct quotation: Louis XIV said, "I am the state."

commas and periods go inside quotes: "Too late," he explained.

colons and semicolons go outside quotes: Ed said, "Hi"; I fled.

title of short story, poem, song: Please sing "Danny Boy."

✎ **title of article, chapter, or part of publication:**
> The third chapter of *My False Demise* is entitled "Rumors."

NOT to indicate cute, trite, or ungrammatical terms:
> Hi, "Buddies," how about a "pep talk!"

Quotation Marks

Pay special attention to the rules involving quotation marks. As you would expect, quotation marks are important in research papers because we include quotations as evidence, so academic writers have to be experts in the correct use of quotation marks. Furthermore, when we say—with quotation marks—that the words enclosed in the quotation marks are what someone else said, then it must be true. There must be no misquotes or deceptive omissions. Our honesty is involved: if we copy someone's words, we use quotation marks (or indent for a long quote), or we are plagiarizing.

There is also a question of how quotation marks are used in conjunction with other marks of punctuation, such as periods and commas. Periods and commas usually go inside quotation marks, "like this," rather than outside them. Semicolons usually go outside "like this"; and so do colons. When we use a parenthetical after a short quotation, we first put closing quotation marks, then the parenthetical, and then the period, "like this" (Thompson 17). If we omit a word or more from a quotation, we indicate the missing words with an ellipsis, "and it looks like a series of three dots . . . like that." If we want to insert a word or more into a quotation, then we do that with brackets, and it [looks] like that. Remember that we do not put quotation marks around long quotations of four lines or more; we indent the entire quotation ten spaces. This meticulous treatment of quotations is an indication of the respect we have for the academic traditions of honor and scholarship. When we quote someone else's intellectual work, we take the trouble to get it right. Notice the ellipsis and brackets in the page below:

Sparrow 1

Jack Sparrow

Dr. Aviary

Biology IH

9 November 2007

The Passerine Finches

The finches are passerine birds, which means that they have feet specially adapted for perching on branches. Edward Gizzard in *Scouting Finches* says that finches "are small but mighty" (Gizzard 42), and in *Getting a Grip* Rachel Chirper says that finches are among the most successful of all terrestrial vertebrates, with "twice as many species as we see in the Rodentia" (Chirper 128). What accounts for the pervasive success of the finches? Does perching itself provide a survival advantage? Chirper points out that:

The fossil record of passerine birds is not extensive because the . . . passerine birds were small, and their bones did not fossilize well, but we see they have inhabited [the planet] since the Eocene. (217)

serine birds are some

apostrophe: (')

    noun made into a possessive: `John's quotation`

    missing letter in a contraction: `don't`

    missing numbers in a year contraction: `'47`

    plurals of letters, numbers, signs, and words as such: *a*'s *5*'s

    with an *s* to show possession after a singular noun: `Dickens's novel`
    Note that singular nouns ending in *s* still add '*s*: `Socrates's philosophy`
    alone to show possession after a plural noun ending in *s*: `dogs'`
    for quotations within quotations:
        `John said, "Hamlet cried, 'Oops!' when he fell."`

    in the contraction of *it* and *is*: `It's a good day to diet.`
    NOT in the possessive pronoun *its*.

    NOT in plural centuries or decades: `1900s   the 50s`

ellipsis: (. . .)

    to indicate words omitted from quotations
    In Courier the ellipsis is made of five spaces and three periods:
        `There are blank spaces between the periods . . . see?`
        `So it looks like this . . . and not like...this.`

    Use three periods if the omission is within a sentence.
    Use four periods if the omission occurs right after a sentence ending;
    the first is the period at the end of the sentence, followed by the ellipsis:
        `Lincoln could not sleep. . . . Douglass spoke first.`

parenthesis: (( ))

    around parenthetical remarks added to a sentence:
        `He said I would be (I wish!) six feet tall.`

brackets: ([ ])

    around words inserted into quoted material:
        `Johnson notes, "At this time [Dickens] began to weaken."`

    When you insert words into quotations, usually for the purpose of clarifying references or enhancing the flow of the sentences, you must enclose your inserted words in brackets like [this] to show that these words were not part of the original quote. Be sure to use true [brackets] rather than (parentheses) or <mathematical symbols>.

The Apostrophe

Serious apostrophe errors are among the most common mistakes that students make. The two most likely locations of apostrophe errors are in possessives and in the contraction of *it* and *is*: *it's*.

First, we make a **singular** noun possessive by adding apostrophe and *s*. This seems simple enough; the possessive of *dog* is *dog's*. The possessive of *Bob* is *Bob's*. But what if the word already ends in *s*, such as *Socrates*? This is where you have to pay strict attention. You still just add the apostrophe and *s* because *Socrates* is singular. So the possessive of *Socrates* is *Socrates's*. If you make the possessive of *Socrates* as *Socrate's*, then you change his name to *Socrate*!

Plural nouns, on the other hand, are different. If you have three dogs, and they have a kennel, then you take the plural noun *dogs* and simply add an apostrophe: *dogs' kennel*. If the plural noun already ends in *s*, then you add the apostrophe. If the plural noun does not already end in *s*, then you can add the apostrophe and *s*, as in the *men's final*.

It's Good to Use *Its* Correctly.

Another apostrophe error that plagues early writing efforts is the *its* error. The word *it's* is the contraction of *it* and *is*. You might say that "It's a good day," or "It's nice to see you." The disaster comes when we write "Give the bird it's food"; but this sentence means, about the bird, that IT IS food. If we do not wish the bird to be food, we should write, "Give the bird its food." The bird will be pleased. The possessive adjective *its* is already possessive and does not contain an apostrophe. There is a prodigious difference in meaning between *it's* and *its*.

In sports we say that you play the way you practice. *It's* the same in grammar and punctuation. If you take the view that you only need to worry about punctuation when you are writing an academic paper, and that you need not think about it the other times you write, you will continuously forget the details. Practice the way you intend to play; make up your mind now that you are going to get apostrophes—including the *it's* apostrophe—right all the time. Punctuation changes meaning. Why say what you do not mean, even in an informal context?

dash: (-- or —)

    A dash is twice as long as a hyphen. Hyphen: - **Dash:** —

✎ **abrupt break in thought:** `So I--wait a minute!--retracted my rebuke.`

✎ **Make a dash in Courier with** `two hyphens, NO spaces--thus.`
    In Times Roman you can make a true dash—like this.
    NOT to replace proper punctuation.

hyphen: (-)

    word divided at end of line
    compound written numbers from twenty-one to ninety-nine
    fractions used as adjectives: `a three-fourths majority`
    prefixes before proper noun or proper adjective: `Pre-Raphaelite`
    compound nouns that include prepositional phrases: `father-in-law`
    compound adjective when it precedes its noun: `a well-meant lie`
    Do NOT use a hyphen (-) **when you intend a dash** (-- or —)
    Do NOT hyphenate an adverb to an adjective: `a completely broken door`

question mark: (?)

    at the end of an interrogative sentence: `Do you have rhubarb?`
    inside closing quotes if part of quote: `He asked, "How about a flower?"`
    outside quotes if not part of quote: `Did he say, "I'll allow it louder"?`

period: (.)

    at the end of a declarative sentence: `I have three words.`
    at the end of a mild imperative sentence: `Please pursue the plot.`
    after most abbreviations: `Dr. Trelawney saw the pirates.`
    inside closing quotation marks: `He said, "Stop that parrot."`

exclamation point: (!)

    after an exclamatory sentence: `The sky is falling!`
    after a strong imperative sentence: `Everyone sit up!`
    NOT to be cute. Wrong: `Hi! Guess what!!`

Learn correct punctuation now, and use it from now on.

The dash—believe me—Is NOT a long-form hyphen.

One of the complications that writing an academic paper creates is having to discern the difference between a **dash** and a **hyphen**. A hyphen is only this - long, but a dash is this — long. Although they have a similar appearance, they are *opposites*; the hyphen glues, and the dash separates. The hyphen pulls together, but the dash pushes apart. The dash is a much longer mark than the hyphen, and you must train your eye to detect the difference in print. Do not put blank spaces on the sides of either one.

    A hyphen is a short-stroke mark. (The term *short-stroke* becomes one word.)

    A dash—see—is a longer mark.

A frequent purpose of the shorter hyphen is to glue two words into a unified, hyphenated term, as when we say that something is a *long-term* problem. In this phrase, *long-term* is a single adjective modifying the noun *problem*. Without the hyphen the adjective *long* stands alone, which changes *term* into a noun: it is a *long term*, and the sentence no longer makes sense. Punctuation affects meaning.

Unlike the hyphen, the dash does not glue words together. The dash indicates a strong interruption to a sentence, as when the interruption is about a different subject altogether: Ladies and gentlemen, I would like to add—Oh, hello Senator—that it is a pleasure to be here. We might also use a dash to show an unfinished sentence if someone is interrupted mid-sentence and never finishes the—.

Our papers will be written in Courier type font, and Courier does not have a real dash, so it is customary to use a double hyphen, without spaces, to indicate a dash in Courier. This means that if you wish to quote a passage that looks like this in a book:

    Lincoln said—as we have elsewhere noted—that he agreed.

In Courier type font you would type the dashes this way, with double hyphens:

```
    Lincoln said--as we have elsewhere noted--that he agreed.
```

USAGE

In Volume One I included a list of common English usage errors. The purpose was not to have you memorize a long list, but to make the book more convenient. Having said that, I will add that this list only lasts a few pages, and you should study it intensely because your goal is to avoid these errors for the rest of your life. Here is the list, but with additional items and special comments on errors that might be problematic or important to academic writing.

✎ To **accept** is to take: I can accept no money for this book.
To **except** is to omit: I can except no one from the rule except Loudon.

Accurate and *precise* are not perfect synonyms. If I say that the book was blue, that might be accurate, but to be precise I would have to say that the book was a pale, sky blue. It is accurate to say that I am nearly six feet tall; it is more precise to say that I am five feet, ten inches tall. A statement can be accurate but still not precise. You want your writing to be *both*.

✎ The verb *affect* means to influence: Your ideas will affect many people.
As a verb, *affect* can mean to pretend: The author affected an English accent.
The adjective *affected* means pretentious or artificial.
The verb *effect* means cause: Your plan will effect a new procedure.
The noun **effect** means result: Your plan will produce a good effect.

✎ **Affect**, not **impact**: It is best to use the word *impact* only as a noun, and not as a verb, in discussing the effect of individuals on history. When we say that x "impacted" y, this usage has an unpleasant medical connotation that is undesirable. The preferable word is *affected*. We affect others, rather than impact them, and when we affect them, this has an impact. The contentious chicken *affected* the others; it did not impact them.

The disturbing use of *impact* as a verb, as in "His attitude impacted me," has grown in popularity. We now hear this solecism (*Solecism* is a wonderful word. Look it up. Seriously.) every day, both in conversation and on television. To an educated ear this usage is particularly revolting because *impacted* refers to intestinal problems and infected wisdom teeth. If you want to discuss a powerful impact, say that the event "had *an impact* on me," not that "it impacted me." Use *impact* as a noun. We certainly do not want you to be impacted, ugh. I hope this note affected you.

Use **afraid of** and **frightened by**, rather than **frightened of**: He was frightened by a moose, and was afraid of them ever since.

Afterward, not **afterwards**: Afterward, the geese came home to roost.

To **aggravate** is to make worse, not to *irritate*; these are not synonyms. It irritated her that she aggravated her cold. In other words we should not say, "That insult aggravated me." The misuse of *aggravate* irritated the literary crowd.

Albeit, not *all be it*: The word *albeit* is a single word which means although. We do not separate it into three words, albeit the dissidents are tempted to.

Use **all right**, not **alright**: We will be all right if the rations arrive.

Use **a lot**, not **alot**: There is no such word as *alot*, just as there is no such word as *abook*.

In formal academic writing, you should avoid **a lot**, even in its correct form. The term is too informal; it belongs in casual conversation, not in a research paper. Instead of *a lot*, use more standard, formal-sounding alternatives, such as *many*, *often*, or *frequently*. Rather than *A lot of geese squawked a lot*; say *Many geese squawked constantly*.

Alumni is plural: The attendees were all alumni. For individuals, a male is an **alumnus**, and a female is an **alumna**. The plural of **alumna** is *alumnae*.

An **allusion** is a reference: His alluded to the hero in the *Iliad*.
An **illusion** is a deception: The bas relief gave the illusion of depth.

We **allude**; we do not **reference**. Horrible: we have begun to hear the noun *reference* used as a verb, as when someone says that "The president referenced the issue in his address." Correct would be that he "referred to the issue," that he alluded to the issue, that he mentioned the issue. *Reference* is a noun; we make **a reference**. This error is important because referring to something is a central process in our research.

Use **and**, not **&**. In ordinary sentences, do not substitute the ampersand (**&**) or the mathematical plus symbol (**+**) for the coordinating conjunction *and*.

Anyway, not **anyways**: Anyway, the Macedonians raised their hands.

Bad is an adjective: The bad decision ruined the bad hatter.
Badly is an adverb: The sturdy Celt did not swim badly.

✎   The reason is not **because**; the reason is **that**: The reason the Visigoths hesitated was *that* they remembered the story of the fox. Use **because** as a subordinating conjunction to begin a dependent clause: Because the Visigoths slept, the Romans crept away.

Something is **between** two: This secret is between you and that Visigoth. Something is **among** three or more: Divide the fish among the five centurions.

We **bring** toward, but we **take** away: If you take someone's shield by mistake, you must bring it back to him.

Can means able to: You can repair a chariot wheel if you know how. **May** means permitted to: Yes, you may repair that chariot.

A **compliment** is a statement of praise: May I compliment your elbow? A **complement** is a supplement: Dessert complemented the citizen's meal.

✎   Not **could of** or **should of**, but **could have** or **should have**: I could have chased pigeons, and I should have chased pigeons. *Of* is a preposition; it is never a helping verb. It is not that you *of* listened; it is that you *have* listened.

Criteria is plural; the singular is **criterion**: There were several criteria, but only one criterion impressed the cynics.

Those criteria: some errors cause special concern, and the misuse of **criteria** is one of them. When we hear someone say that a detail "is an important criteria," we lose confidence in the opinion at once. *Criteria* is plural, so how could someone pretending to be an expert in a set of criteria not know even the main word? There are many criteria, but only one critical **criterion**. This usage question is more likely than most to come up in your writing, as is the use of the plural **data** below.

Currently means now; **presently** means soon: The citizens want corn currently, but they will have to settle for getting it presently.

Curricula is plural; the singular is **curriculum**: Our curricula need revising, especially our curriculum on the lives of citizens.

The noun **data** is plural and requires a plural verb: These data are not encouraging the scholars. *Datum* is the singular. We are beginning to see some acceptance of *data* as a singular noun, but for now, treat it as plural.

Different from, not **different than**: The oar was different from the others.

Disinterested means without prejudice because of having no personal interest in something: We need a disinterested judge to try this case fairly. **Uninterested** means without interest in the sense of being bored: The thief was uninterested in the disinterested judge. We see this error often, unfortunately.

Use **done** only with a helping verb: I **have done** nothing to the table. We would never say, "I done it."

Don't is the contraction of "do not": We don't like duplicity.
Doesn't is the contraction of "does not": He doesn't like domesticity.
Don't use **don't** for third person: Wrong: He don't like laxity.

Due to modifies nouns: The collapse is due to faulty concrete.
Because of modifies verbs: The bridge collapsed because of iron oxidation.

To **emigrate** is to migrate out: The dissident emigrated from Russia.
To **immigrate** is to migrate in: The artist immigrated to Puerto Rico.
Emigrants leave, immigrants arrive.

Everyone and **everybody** are singular: Everyone has his or her own mind.
NOT: Everyone has *their* own mind.

Notice that we do not say, "Everyone are here." Although it might at first seem to be a plural word, **everyone** is singular. In fact, all of these words are singular: **everybody**, **anybody**, **anyone**, **each**, **neither**, **nobody**, and **someone**. Notice a critical consequence of the fact that they are singular: you cannot say "Everyone has *their* coat," or "Someone dropped *their* hat." **Everyone** is not THEY; it is singular. Everyone has his or her coat. Someone dropped his or her hat. If that sounds too mechanical, then shift to "Someone dropped a hat."

Use **farther** for distance: Her baseball went farther than his went.
Use **further** for time: We will consider this question further.

Use **feel bad** rather than **feel badly**: The victim felt bad.

Use **fewer** for countable things: There are fewer Visigoths.
Use **less** for uncountable amounts: There is less sugar for the citizens.

If you are enumerating elements in your essay, use **first** and **second**, rather than *firstly* and *secondly*. The latter terms with their *-ly* suffix have a supercilious, pedantic ring to them that is undesirable.

Fortuitous means by chance: A fortuitous circumstance affected them.
Fortunate means lucky: A fortunate condition benefitted them.

Good is an adjective: The good swimmer swam her fastest time.
Well is usually an adverb: The good swimmer swam well.
Well can sometimes be an adjective: He is not a well man.

It is worth a moment to discuss **good** versus **well**. The crux of the matter is the verb, *feel*. If you feel carefully in the darkness to find your keys, then *feel* is an action verb. But *feel* is often a linking verb, as in *I feel good*. In that sentence *I* is the subject, *feel* is the linking verb, and *good* is an adjective subject complement modifying *I*. If you say *I feel well*, that either means that you are adept at feeling objects, or that you do not feel sick.

Clothes, when put out to dry, are **hung**. People, when strung up to die, are **hanged**. The conspirators in Lincoln's assassination were hanged.

Hopefully is an adverb meaning "full of hope"; it should not be used as a substitute for "I hope." To say "Hopefully, I can go," is an error. I hope this teaches them a lesson. I am hopeful that it will. I think hopefully about that possibility.

Ideas are concepts or thoughts. We could discuss the philosophical ideas of Friedrich Nietzsche. **Ideals** are standards of perfection.

To **imply** is to suggest: He implied that Visigoths were to blame.
To **infer** is to deduce: We inferred that Visigoths were being blamed.

Infer versus **imply**: here is another choice that might cause problems in a formal paper because you will be attempting to show what data mean, so you might say something ridiculous such as, "These events infer that a danger does exist." Events cannot infer; they have no minds. People infer. We infer when we make an *infer*ence, when we deduce a conclusion from the facts. We imply when we suggest something without stating it directly. To say, "He inferred that I was an incompetent clown" would be wrong; you mean that he implied it.

It's is the contraction of **it is**: It's fun to understand Stanley.
Its is a possessive adjective or pronoun: The dog ate its food, growling.

Use **kind of** rather than **kind of a**: It seemed to be some kind of artifact.

Use **lend** as a verb: Lend me money for a cloak.
Use **loan** as a noun: Give me a loan for a day.

To **lie** (v.i.) is to rest: I will lie in the shade near the field.
To **lay** (v.t.) is to put: I will lay the hammer near the centurion.

Use **like** to compare nouns and pronouns; as a preposition that indicates similarity: We have good shields like these.
Use **as** as a conjunction to introduce a clause: We have shields, as you have.
Use **such as** to show examples: He had enemies, such as Alaric the Visigoth.

Literally means actually, not figuratively. You could say, "We literally left within two minutes," but not, "We literally vanished." If the shield did not really physically vanish, poof, then the shield did not literally vanish.

Through some bizarre twist of fate, the misuse of **literally** has become popular, even pervasive, and this misuse reverses meaning; it causes people to say **literally** when they mean not literally! **Literally** means really; **literally** does not imply that what you state is a figure of speech. It does not imply a similarity but an actuality. People say things such as, "It rained so hard, the sky literally fell." What? If the sky literally fell, there would be a mighty crash and great blue flakes all over the ground. If a wound literally heals before your eyes, that means that the wound closes and heals in seconds as you watch, as in a supernatural process. If you mean that the wound healed extremely well in a normal way, then you may not say that it healed literally before your eyes because that is not true. If you write a paper on the giant squid, you must not say that the oceans are literally full of them; that would mean LITERALLY full, as in nothing but squid, everywhere you look.

In the past we used the terms **man** and **mankind**, and even the possessive adjective/pronoun **his**, to refer to all human beings, both male and female. Today, our sensitivities have improved, and we avoid defaulting to the masculine gender when we express something that includes women. Other terms, such as **human beings**, **humanity**, **persons**, and even the compound pronouns such as **his or her** sound more accurate and more aware.

Myself and **yourself** should be used as reflexive or intensive pronouns rather than as direct objects. "I, myself, believed the Visigoth" is correct usage, but "She asked John and myself if we had the chariot" is not. It would be correct to say, "She asked John and me if we had the chariot."

Nauseous means sickening: The outcome was nauseous to us.
Nauseated means sick at the stomach: The seasick citizen was nauseated.

In other words, if I say "I am nauseous," it means I make *you* sick. When my stomach is upset, I am nauseated, not nauseous.

Number is for countables: There were a number of citizens present.
Amount is for uncountables: There was an enormous amount of tension.

Use **off** rather than **off of**: The ball bounced off the backboard.

Use **more than**, not **over; over** is the opposite of **under**; it means above or on top of; it does not mean *more than*. There were more than six citizens but fewer than nine.

People, not **persons**: The plural of *person* is *people*. The weary citizen waited for the people, but only one person arrived.

Phenomenon is singular and **phenomena** is plural: The weirdest phenomenon was the way the donkeys ran in circles.

Phenomena is another error that might show up in a research paper. Educated speakers know that *phenomena* is plural; they would never (EVER) say that "This is an interesting phenomena." There is no such thing as "a phenomena"; that would be like "a ducks." Say "a phenome**non**." Something can be an interesting phenomenon, or there can be many strange phenomena. Miss this one and you have to go to time-out.

Save **plus** for mathematics and use **in addition to** or **also** instead.

Precipitate means hasty, and **precipitous** means steep.

Use **reason**, not **reason why**: This is the reason fortunes decline.

Reference is a noun. **Refer** is a verb. You cannot reference something; you refer to it.

Regardless, not **irregardless**. There is no such word as *irregardless*.

The phrase **relate to** is a vague colloquialism. Instead of saying that many people relate to J.D. Salinger's character Holden Caulfield, say that many people understand Holden, or that they find that Holden's struggles remind them of their own struggles.

Use **raise** transitively: The crew will attempt to raise the Titanic.
Use **rise** intransitively: The mist began to rise slowly through the air.

Real means actual: The real criminal escaped.
Wrong: The citizen was real tired.
Really means very: The Visigoth was really tall.

Respectfully is with respect: He spoke respectfully of his family.
Respectively is in sequence: He spoke of his father, his brother, and his sister, respectively.

Use **since** rather than **seeing as how**: Since my grandfather died, I have had many wonderful memories of him.

Another issue involving **since** is that we sometimes use *since* when we mean *because*, as in "Since you disagree, I will not proceed." The problem is that *since* is best used to indicate a passage of time, as in "I have not eaten well since Rudolph glowed." If you mean *because*, it is best to say *because*, and keep *since* for periods of time.

You **sit** (v.i.) down in a chair: She was sitting there near the fire.
You **set** (v.t.) down a book: She was setting the provisions on the ice.

Someone is not they. We saw this issue earlier; here is a reminder. Rather than saying, "Someone dropped *their* shield," say, "Someone dropped a shield." Use **they** or **their** only if you mean a group of people.

You **teach** people, and you **learn** subjects: you do NOT learn people things. You can teach a horse to drink, but you cannot learn one to drink.

Than is a conjunction: We have more provisions than you have.
Then is an adverb: We will go now; you go then.

Them should be used as an object pronoun, not as an adjective. Wrong: And so, my friends, ask not when you can have them provisions.

They're is the contraction of "they are": They're feeding rhinos grits.
Their is a possessive adjective: They're feeding their giraffes.
There is a place: They're feeding their elephants there.

To is a preposition or an infinitive: She went to Boston to collect stones.
Too is an adverb meaning "also" or "too much": I sleep too much, too.
Two is a number: Two attendants twisted twine in the twilight.

They're-their-there and **to-too-two** are among the most common serious errors of early writing. Because these are homophones, words that sound exactly the same, these errors can persist, even in rough drafts by advanced writers. The difference is that an advanced writer knows these errors well, takes them seriously, and catches them in the proofreading process. They do not remain in submitted work. These are regarded as elementary, school-child errors, and to make them in formal paper is an embarrassment. If you want to rid your writing of these, remember that you play the way you practice; you tend to do things the way you are used to doing them. If you think these errors are unimportant when you write informal language, and you pay little attention most of the time, you will be far more likely to make them when you write academic papers.

Toward, not **towards**: The silent citizen moved slowly toward the exit.

Use **try to** rather than **try and**: Please try to help the citizen.

Something is either **unique**—one of a kind—or not. There are no degrees of uniqueness, so nothing can be *very* unique. The Grand Canyon is unique.

Use **use**, not **utilize**: He used a plastic owl to startle the pigeons.

Use **way off** rather than **ways off**: He was a long way off from the walls.

Do not use **-wise** as a suffix. Wrong: It was a bad day, foodwise, for citizens.

Who is a subject pronoun: Who is with the guest?
Whom is an object pronoun: To whom do you wish to give the chisel?

Who refers to people: It was they who followed the crowd.
That and **which** refer to objects: Camels ate the grass that remained.

Who's is the contraction of *who* and *is*: Who's going to ask the citizen?
Whose is a pronoun or adjective: Whose words these are, I think I know.

On the following page there are ten usage errors hidden in a sample page about Alexander the Great. The legend about Alexander is a real legend, and the three ancient historians are real, but the modern authors I cite are invented. Can you find all ten errors?

Proofreading Practice: Find Ten Usage Errors

It is easy to look straight at an error and not see it. Hurrying makes things worse.

Sponse 1

1   Audrey Sponse

2   Ms. Reeding

3   History IH

4   9 April 2009

5   Issus and Alexander's Capture of Sisygambis

6   Among the very unique stories from ancient history is Alexander the

7   Great's capture of Sisygambis, the mother of Darius III, King of Persia, at

8   the Battle of Issus in 333 B.C. According to the legend, Darius fled the

9   battlefield, leaving alot of his family to the mercy of the Macedonians,

10   but Alexander, who was a military phenomena, treated Sisygambis with great

11   respect and courtesy, ordering his soldiers to treat her as royalty. When

12   she was later informed that Darius had died, she replied, "I have only one

13   son [Alexander], and he is king of Persia" (Marley 73). Sisygambis remained

14   with Alexander until his death, and then, unable to endure Alexander's

15   death, she had herself walled-in to her room and died in a few days. The

16   question is, how much of this legend is true? Are there ancient sources

17   that confirm the legend, factwise?

18   Our best knowledge of Alexander comes from five ancient accounts, of

19   which the three earliest are by Diodorus Siculus, Justin, and Curtius.

20   Maria Rodriguez, professor of ancient history at Cornwell University,

21   references Curtius's account as most accurate:

22   Curtius established connections among other ancient sources for

23   the details that he presented. If not for Curtius's account of

24   the capture of Sisygambis, we would not have the details about

25   the death of Sisygambis. (Rodriguez 106)

26   Since Curtius utilized multiple sources--like modern historians

27   do--to confirm details, he was able to report facts with confidence. Although

28   Curtius could of simply told the story, he cited over ten sources in his

GRAMMAR RULES AND ERRORS

In Volume One I explained ten common grammar problems. Here they are again, expanded and supplemented with five more. I have included standard proofreader's marks in blue. There is some overlap between these and the usage errors, and there will be overlap between these and the archived research paper comments. The overlap is fine; it will do us good to look at these details a few times in a few ways.

Subject / Verb Disagreement   s/v

The subject/verb disagreement is the worst error in grammar. The subject of each sentence will be either singular or plural, and the verb must agree with it in number. If the subject is singular, the verb must be singular.

> Wrong: The reason for the numerous objections are obvious.

> Right: The reason for the numerous objections is obvious.

The most common reason for a subject/verb disagreement is the presence of intervening words between the subject and the verb, as in the two examples above. Compound subjects joined by *and* are plural: Bob and Jane are here; compound subjects joined by *or* are singular: Bob or Jane is here. When a gerund phrase is the subject, the verb agrees with the gerund, not the object of the gerund, as in: "*Defeating* the Persians *is* the purpose of the invasion."

Spelling Error   sp

With word processors and spell checkers so prevalent, there is no excuse for a spelling error in the final draft of an academic paper. Some spelling errors, however, are surprisingly common, including two shockers: a spelling error in the title of your paper, and the misspelling of your main word, such as spelling *Iliad Illiad* in a paper about *The Iliad*. It never occurs to us that we are misspelling our title or our main word, so we do not think to double-check those.

> Wrong: Shakespear: The Tragic Genius.

> Right: Shakespeare: The Tragic Genius.

The task is not to learn hundreds of errors; it is to learn a handful perfectly. Concentrate.

Sentence Fragment *frag*

Advanced academic writing is made of complete sentences. Groups of words that do not make complete thoughts are errors, called *fragments*. One common sentence fragment is to put a period after an introductory dependent clause.

Wrong: When scientists photographed the squid. They were amazed.

Right: When scientists photographed the squid, they were amazed.

Another common sentence fragment occurs when you put a period after an introductory participial phrase:

Wrong: Catching the full force of the gale. Robert crouched.

Right: Catching the full force of the gale, Robert crouched.

Run-On Sentence R-S

A compound sentence joined by a coordinating conjunction must have a comma before the conjunction, or else it is a run-on sentence.

Wrong: The sun began to rise and they saw the extent of the damage.

Right: The sun began to rise, and they saw the extent of the damage.

Comma Splice CS

A comma splice occurs when a comma, rather than a semicolon or comma and coordinating conjunction, is used to connect two independent clauses.

Wrong: The old man reeled in the fish, the sun began to set.

Right: The old man reeled in the fish, and the sun began to set.

Right: The old man reeled in the fish; the sun began to set.

Bad Appositive Construction

An appositive is an interrupting definition. It provides important information immediately, so the reader does not have to read on in confusion. The danger is that appositives must be enclosed in commas—one to start the definition, and one to return to the main idea. If we forget the second comma, we can completely change the meaning of the sentence.

Wrong: Robert, the mailman is stealing our car.

Right: Robert, the mailman, is stealing our car.

Notice that in the first sentence there are two men, and we are speaking to Robert. In the second sentence there is one man, and the person being spoken to is not named. The absence of the second appositive comma wreaked all that havoc.

Pronoun Case *pron*

Subjects and subject complements must use subject pronouns. Direct objects, indirect objects, objects of prepositions, and objects of verbals must use object pronouns. *A subject is a subject, and an object is an object.*

> Wrong: It will be important to you and I.
>
> Right: It will be important to you and me.

Pronoun Reference *ref*

When multiple nouns precede a pronoun, the antecedent of the pronoun can become unclear. This is called a *reference* error.

> Wrong: James suddenly encountered John, and he looked startled.
>
> Right: James suddenly encountered John, and John looked startled.

Pronoun Number: A *They-Their* Error *ref*

The pronouns *they* and *their* are plural, not singular. When something is *theirs*, then it belongs to a group. Something belonging to an individual is *his* or *hers*.

> Wrong: One of the poets dropped their book.
>
> Right: One of the poets dropped a book.

Misplaced Modifier *mm*

An introductory participial phrase must be set off by a comma and must modify the grammatical subject of the sentence. The modifier is misplaced if the intended target word is present in the sentence, but the modifier modifies the wrong word because of its placement.

> Wrong: Barking furiously at the mailman, Susan shushed Fido.
>
> Right: Barking furiously at the mailman, Fido angered Susan.

Dangling Modifier *DGL or dgl*

A dangling modifier occurs when the intended target word is not even present in the sentence at all.

> Wrong: Barking furiously at the mailman, the day was off to a bad start.
>
> Right: Barking furiously at the mailman, Fido woke us up.

Split Infinitive *We would use the delete mark to remove the inserted word.*
We regard an infinitive as a single word. In advanced academic writing we do not split the infinitive with an adverb.

> Wrong: Roosevelt began to slowly develop economic programs.
> Right: Slowly, Roosevelt began to develop economic programs.

Parallel lists and compounds //
Lists and compounds need to be constructed with parallel grammar. A list should consist of all adjectives or all nouns, but not a mixture.

> Wrong: Dickens was a novelist, a poet, and spoke often.
> Right: Dickens was a novelist, a poet, and a frequent speaker.

Parallel Tense t
Tenses should not wander; they should be logical. If you are describing the past, stay in past tense.

> Wrong: Jefferson went home. Soon he is building again.
> Right: Jefferson went home. Soon he was building again.

Double Negative
Many languages, such as Spanish, accept double negatives as a way to intensify an idea, but we do not use double negatives in standard English.

> Wrong: Dickens did *not* know *nothing* about the event.
> Wrong: I am *not* accusing *nobody*.
> Right: Dickens knew nothing about the event.
> Right: I am not accusing anyone.

See if you can find hidden grammar or usage errors in the sample paper on the next two pages. This paper, because of these errors, is severely flawed and would not receive a passing grade in my class. This is a shame because the ideas in the paper are interesting, but their expression is ruined by these basic errors, and the paper is disorganized. I have added line numbers, in blue, to help you discuss what you find.

Study and reread these until you understand each error and remember its name.

Proofreading Practice: Find Grammar, Usage, Punctuation, and Spelling Errors

Mallow 1

1   Marsha Mallow

2   Ms. Enscene

3   English Honors II

4   11 May 2009

5   The Wild Surmise of Negative Capabilaty

6   The English poet John Keats (1795-1821) is regarded as one of the

7   geniuses of English poetry. It is said that on an October evening in 1816,

8   after his friend Charles Cowden Clarke showed him the Elizabethan playwright

9   George Chapman's new translation of *The Iliad*, Keats was able to actually

10 compose a Petrarchan sonnet (with rhyme scheme abbaabbacdcdcd), "On First

11 Looking into Chapman's Homer," during his walk home. Clarke had Keats's

12 now-famous poem on his desk by ten o'clock the next morning.

13   In Keats's sonnet the narrator reads Chapman's translation and is as

14 astonished as he would be if a new planet were discovered (Uranus had been

15 rediscovered by William Herschel in 1781) or as astonished as Cortez (Keats

16 confused Cortez and Balboa) was in 1513 upon discovering the Pacific Ocean.

17   Writing brilliant poetry, astonishment is a central element of Keats's

18 poetic thought. Keats is known for his aesthetic theory of *negative*

19 *capability*, an idea that pervades his poetry and that is important in his

20 sonnet about Chapman's Homer. He first articulated the idea in 1817 in a

21 letter to his brothers, George and Thomas Keats; he wrote:

22   . . . at once it struck me, what quality went to form a Man

23   of Achievement especially in literature & which Shakespeare

24   possessed so enormously--I mean Negative Capability, that is

25   when man is capable of being in uncertainties, Mysteries, doubts

26   without any irritable reaching after fact & reason. (Keats 48)

27   Negative capability, the lack of the irritating need for certainties,

28 have been described as a "state of intentional open-mindedness" (Ratz 94).

29 The universe, Keats seems to say, is permanently beyond our complete

30 comprehension, and individuals of "achievement" will be at peace with

31 the reality of mystery. Perplexing humanity, Keats felt that "poets,

32 particularly, live in the presence of uncertainty" (Keats 153).

33   Keats's deep respect for the world's unknowns are not, of course,

34 unique. In the western intellectual tradition, the respect for perplexity

35 traces back to Socrates as portrayed in Plato's *Dialogues*. In Plato's

36 "Apology" Socrates explains to the jury of Athenians (who would soon find

37 him guilty of believing in false gods and corrupting the youth) that he

38 was surprised when the Oracle of Delphi "proclaimed him the wisest man in

39 Athens. On the contrary, Socrates explained, he only knew that he knew

40 nothing" (Adams 48). Socratic perplexity has had wide acceptance among

41 great thinkers. The great German poet Goethe, a contemporary of Keats once

42 said that "Doubt increases with knowledge" (Worthwords 119).

43   In "On First Looking into Chapman's Homer" we see the presence of

44 negative capability in the final three lines of the sonnet. Believing that

45 the Atlantic Ocean separates Europe from Asia. Cortez and his men have

46 climbed the mountain in Darien (Panama), expecting to see the vast Chinese

47 landscape. Instead, they see the vast Pacific Ocean, and they slowly realize

48 that they are standing on an unknown back side of the planet. Keats

49 compares Chapman's *Iliad* to the discovery, when "stout Cortez when with

50 eagle eyes / He star'd at the Pacific--and all his men / Look'd at each other

51 with a wild surmise-- / Silent, upon a peak in Darien" (11-14).

52   This silent, wild surmise is a moment of negative capability, a moment

53 of astonishment for Cortez (Balboa) and his men and it is the same wild

54 surmise that Keats felt upon reading George Chapman's translation. Until

55 that moment, Homer had been only a famous name for Keats; he "had been told

56 / That deep-browed Homer" (5-6) ruled the domain of poetry, but he had not

Notice how distracting it is when there are many errors. Proofreading matters.

GRADING: FOUR CORE ELEMENTS

As I explained in Volume One, grading practices vary widely from school system to school system and from teacher to teacher. Some schools do not assign letter or number grades, hoping to focus on progress and positive experience. Some teachers apply mathematical point systems to student writing in an effort to be objective and fair. Some teachers implement extensive writing rubrics to chart the presence or absence of an array of details. Some teachers minimize the correction of English errors, feeling that emphasizing mistakes is demoralizing. There is no one grading philosophy that dominates academic practice.

In this program I cannot and do not wish to impose my own grading philosophy on anyone. There are too many variables that make one situation different from another, so I cannot tell you that one method is right and another is wrong. What I can do is explain what you will face in advanced high school and college courses, and explain the grading system you would face if you were writing papers for me. This is certain: however leniently you may be graded now, you will face strict grading standards if you continue in academics.

In Volume One I explained my grading method in detail, so here I will provide only a summary. While I understand the good intentions and goals of many grading systems more lenient than mine, I have always taken a tough and simple approach to grading formal papers. Here are the core principles:

I think that the language of grading should be the same as the language of writing. I do not want to use a separate grading language or to put numbers on a paper. I do not want grading charts, checklists, or rubrics. I think that grading should have a literary, rather than a mathematical, tone. I do not want to add *any thinking process that a real writer would not use*; instead, I want to grade based on four **core elements**, the few clear principles that real writers use: correct **English**, correct **format** (MLA, in this case), good **essay** structure, and good evidence for a meaningful **thesis**. I think students should think about writing the same way that professional writers think about writing.

When I grade a paper, I cannot worry that a low grade will hurt a student's feelings. We must trust each other. If the grade is bad, it will hurt my feelings too, but this knowledge is too important; you must know the truth now if you are to write well in college. We both have to be professional and grown-up about the grade. If you want to master academic writing, you have to know what you are doing wrong. The truth is the fastest, most honest, and most respectful path.

I use standard proofreading symbols and marginal notes to mark errors as I read the paper. Then I type a letter, including explanations of the errors, and paste it to the front of the student's paper. The grade is based on this simple sequence:

Standard English for a D.

To pass, the paper must be written in standard English; this is not negotiable. I can forgive a few errors that slip by your proofreading process, but if I have to correct five or ten errors per page, then the paper cannot even receive a D. I do not want to play games with writing; if I tolerate elementary errors that students should have mastered years ago, all is lost. Academic writing means caring deeply about quality; it is time to bear down, review the English standards, proofread intensely, and get your English right.

Plus Correct MLA Format for a C.

To receive a C, the paper must have standard English and also correct MLA format. A slight problem or two is understandable, but if the paper is not essentially in correct MLA format, I will not give it a C.

Plus Essay Structure for a B.

To receive a B, the paper must have standard English, MLA format, and excellent essay structure. It must have a good introduction, body, and conclusion, all centered on a clear thesis. It must be tied together coherently.

Plus Good Ideas for an A.

To receive an A, the paper must have all of the above, and also have a meaningful, interesting thesis that is supported by good quotations and facts. It must be worth reading.

REAL RESEARCH PAPER COMMENTS

In Volume One I showed forty real research paper comments that I had put on student papers over a period of years. When I would write, for example, an explanation of a run-on sentence error for a student, I would save it in my computer, so that the next time a student made the same error, I could easily copy and paste the explanation. During a period of years, I gradually archived and refined several hundred comments. This archive of real comments is important because it reveals the kinds of errors (or accomplishments) students really make. In Volume Two I will introduce forty more comments, but here are the forty from Volume One for your review. Review these with great care because in Volume Two I assume that you *already understand* these points.

1. A discussion of ideas, not just a report.
One of the advanced features of your paper is that the paper is not a mere report; it is a display of your reasoning. You do not limit yourself to the role of reporter, humbly displaying other people's statements; instead, you structure your paper as an argument, a display of your own ideas in which you use facts and expert comment to support what you say. That is excellent.

2. Good proofreading.
One of the best features of your work is the excellent proofreading you have done. This makes your paper free of the irritating elementary errors that distract a reader's attention away from ideas. Advanced polish and detail like this makes your paper pleasant to read; it brings your thoughts to the fore.

3. Well-chosen quotations.
A quality that distinguishes your paper is your excellent selection of material for quotation. These well-chosen quotations lend force and cogency to your argument. They also provide the reader with extremely interesting passages to read, and they show a high level of comprehension on your part.

4. Use proper paragraphs. ¶
Use proper paragraphs. The paragraph symbol ¶ means that you should have indented five spaces to start the next paragraph. Be sure to paragraph your work properly. Usually, begin a new paragraph after a long quotation.

5. Your conclusion is listy.
Your conclusion contains many good things, but they are not organized well, separated clearly, tied together revealingly, or expressed surprisingly. It reads like a list of repetitions of things you said before. I want you to concentrate on the art of writing a convincing conclusion that will impress, interest, inform, and convince a reader.

6. Your conclusion is undeveloped.

Please write a carefully developed conclusion. Now that you have shown the reader all of the evidence for your thesis, it is time to show what the evidence means; you cannot expect the reader to remember everything and total it all up for himself. You cannot expect the reader to draw the conclusions; you have to do it. Review the most important ideas, but do not just repeat the headlines from the body. Do not just go back over things you have already said. In the conclusion, go to a new height. Take the time to pull themes together, to highlight relationships, and to synthesize all of the information into a final recognition. Do not introduce new themes, but show the implications and the interrelations of the various ideas previously explored in your paper. Remember that the conclusion is your first real chance to discuss everything because it is not until the conclusion that the reader has finally been presented with all of the facts and ideas that appeared in the body.

7. Clarify your paragraphs' relationships.

At times in your paper I had difficulty understanding how what I was reading related to what I had just read. The reader needs to know the logical status of each paragraph. Is it another example supporting what was said in the previous paragraph? Is this a contrasting idea? Have we begun a completely new section of the paper? How, exactly, does this idea relate to the thesis? In beginning each paragraph, you need to write something that will show the reader the relationship of this paragraph to the previous paragraph and to the thesis. Like an essay, a paragraph needs an introduction, even if it only consists of a few connecting words, such as "Another reason that Euripides was condemned by Aristophanes was . . . " You might even need an entire connecting paragraph just to clarify the relationship between the previous several paragraphs and the following several paragraphs.

8. You have a sentence fragment. (frag)

Please write in complete sentences, avoiding sentence fragments. My proofreader's mark *frag* indicates the presence in your paper of a sentence fragment, one of the most serious grammar errors. It is essential, in a formal research paper, to write in complete sentences. There must be a subject, a predicate, and a complete thought in every sentence you write. Common types of sentence fragments include: 1) Dependent clauses punctuated as though they were sentences: "When Melville went to sea. His real adventure had begun." 2) Participial phrases punctuated as though they were sentences: "After deserting the ship. Melville lived among cannibals." 3) Verbless subject and appositive clusters: "Herman Melville, a seafaring author." 4) Subjectless predicates: "Melville arrived. Went to the Inn." 5) Groups of confused words: "Melville in the seafaring adventure cannibals." 6) Fragments caused by using quotations in a way that fails to complete the thought: "Spencer believed that social struggle 'for existence as leading to the perfect society.'" 7) The "being" fragment, in which you mistake the word "being" for a verb: "Dante described nine circles of the Inferno. The first circle being Limbo."

9. Your thesis word is misspelled. (sp)

Spell your key words correctly! A surprisingly common and embarrassing error is to misspell the key word of the paper. An example would be to misspell *Shakespear* in a paper about Shakespeare, to spell *Iliad Illiad*, to write a paper about Thoreau's *Walden* and spell it *Waldon*, or to write a paper about Jonathan Swift and spell his name *Jonathon*.

10. You have a misplaced modifier. (mm)

Avoid misplaced modifiers. My *mm* mark means that you have a misplaced modifier, a serious error in grammar. You must develop a sense of modifier placement. Words, phrases, and even clauses that act as modifiers must be placed next to or as close as possible to the things they modify. If you put the modifier somewhere else, it will modify something else, and the result is often nonsense. Some examples: If you say that "In an effort to be modest, Whitman's first edition of poetry lacked his name," that means that the book was being modest--a ridiculous idea. To correct the modification error, place the modifier next to the word you really intend to modify: "In an effort to be modest, Whitman omitted his name from the first edition of his poetry." The sentence, "An idealist, most of Plato's ideas are only ideals" means that ideas are idealists! Better would have been, "An idealist, Plato regarded his ideas as ideals." "Feeling alone and desperate, this was one of Dinesen's last letters" means that a letter felt desperate. Correct would have been, "Feeling alone and desperate, Dinesen wrote one of her last letters." Modifiers are like lights; they illuminate things close to them, and so you have to put them next to their intended targets.

11. Your MLA details are excellent

I really appreciate the excellent job you have done of following the MLA format. Your first page, your documentary technique, your margins and spacing, and your Works Cited listings all show advanced attention to detail. This gives me, as a reader, more time to spend thinking about your ideas.

12. Good clause punctuation

You have done a good job punctuating the clauses in your sentences. I do not see any run-on sentences or comma splices in the paper. Attention to clauses makes a big difference in how clear and understandable your paper is.

13. Connect the sections of your essay.

When you write the paragraphs and sections of your paper, you must write connecting language--usually at the beginning of each paragraph--which show the reader that you have left the previous idea behind and that you are now moving to a different idea that is related to the previous idea in a specific way. You have to write both the sections and the connections. Otherwise, the paper is like the pieces of a model that have not yet been glued together.

14. You have a pronoun case error (pron)

It is important to apply the rule for pronoun case: a subject is a subject and an object is an object. In other words, the clause subject and the subject complement both take subject pronouns, but the direct object, indirect object, and object of preposition must all take object pronouns. Alexander felt a rivalry between HIM and his father, NOT between HE and his father--the object of preposition must use an object pronoun.

15. The proofreading is inadequate.

I am sorry to have to emphasize that this paper shows a serious lack of editing and proofreading. You simply have not taken the time to perfect the details of spelling, punctuation, or grammar. You must understand that proofreading is not a brief concluding activity; it is a methodical, detailed, time-consuming, professional process in which you rid your paper of elementary errors. You will have to change your proofreading methods if you are to write advanced papers. Whatever method you are presently using to make sure that your paper is ready to turn in, stop doing that, and do something different.

16. You have a subject/verb disagreement (s/v)

Always make your verbs agree with your subjects. My mark s/v indicates subject/ verb disagreement, one of the most serious and embarrassing errors of grammar. Remember that your verb must always agree with, and ONLY WITH, the subject of the sentence--no matter what else comes between the subject and the verb, such as intervening adverbs or prepositional phrases that make you forget what subject you are matching your verb to. Also remember that certain pronouns are always singular, such as *each*, *someone*, *somebody*, *everyone*, and *everybody*. Notice the subject/verb disagreement in the following sentence: "Each of his stories contain some philosophical view." Each/contain should be corrected to Each/contains.

17. A special subject/verb problem: the OP Trap

Your paper indicates that you need to review the rule: do not match your verb to the object of a preposition! See the disagreement in the following sentence: "Dostoevsky's views on ethics is best summed up . . . ." The intervening prepositional phrase *on ethics* distracts your mind from the real subject of the sentence, *views*, and you wind up saying views/is rather than views/are. We see the same problem in this sentence: "The tone of Aristotle's writings were different." Tone/was, not tone/were. The subject is not *writings*, it is *tone*. Or: "The impact of Plato's ideas are present in the world today." Impact/ is. Or: "Two of the major themes in *Don Quixote* was humor and irony." Two/ were. Or: "The popularity of Pasternak's political struggles have overshadowed the quality of his novel." Popularity/has. Beware of intervening material, especially prepositional phrases; the subject must agree with the verb. Always find the real subject as you write your verb.

Notice that if the subject and verb do not agree, then your sentence is contradicting itself because one is indicating that the idea is about something singular, while the other is indicating that the idea is about something plural. This means that the fundamental idea of your sentence is nonsense!

18. You have spelling errors. (sp)

One unacceptable problem in your paper, as you see, is that you have numerous spelling errors, which are not acceptable at this level of academic work. It is your responsibility to use a dictionary until every word in your paper is spelled correctly. Do not be lazy about using a dictionary; if you think a word is probably spelled correctly, you can be sure that it is not. I have placed the *sp* proofreader's mark beside spelling errors. Please do whatever you must to rid your papers of spelling errors in the future.

19. Please transpose these elements. (tr)

My *tr* mark means that you have words or letters that are out of order and that need to be transposed back into the order in which they belong. I would place a *tr* mark beside misspellings such as *thier* or beside awkward constructions such as "Then became he indignant." I would also do this if you wrote "Alighieri Dante" because *Dante* is the first name, and *Alighiere* is the last name.

20. Avoid exaggeration.

Beware of exaggerated claims and unsupported generalities. If you claim that "no other author has ever" done something, what is your evidence? Are you prepared to discuss the work of every other author and demonstrate its inadequacy? The "most people" error also falls in this category. If you claim that most people think x, do you have evidence in the form of polls or statistics or even quotations from social science that a majority of people think x, or are you just exaggerating? In a formal paper you do not guess or exaggerate; your statements are expected to be the truth; accurate and defensible just as they are expressed.

21. You have a pronoun reference error: THIS as the subject.

Please avoid using the demonstrative pronoun *this* as the subject of a sentence. Use it as an adjective, referring to *this idea*, *this policy*, *this poem*. When you just say "this altered everything," there is almost always ambiguity, leaving the reader to wonder what this you mean.

22. You have a compound subject/verb disagreement. s/v

You have a subject/verb disagreement caused by a compound subject. Remember that a compound subject joined by *and* is plural because it means both: Smith and Jones write. A compound subject joined by *or* is singular because it means only one: Smith or Jones writes. A compound subject joined by *or* but that contains a plural noun as the second subject is plural: Smith or the Joneses are here. As a fundamental principal of grammar, the verb must always agree with the subject.

23. You have a title spelling error. sp

My mark *sp* means that you have a spelling error. Certain spelling errors are remarkably common, including misspelling of the main word of the paper and in the title of the paper, or in the first paragraph, because it never occurs to you that you could make a spelling error so obvious or so soon! Always double-check your title and main word.

24. You have a split infinitive.

It is best to word your sentences as to avoid split infinitives. Splitting an infinitive means inserting an adverb between the two words of the infinitive form of a verb. If we take the infinitive *to see*, and split it with the adverb *vividly*, we have *to vividly see*, which is a split infinitive. It is better to put the adverb after the infinitive: *to see vividly*. Instead of writing that Aristophanes's criticism allowed Athenians "to not only see that he was a better writer," write "not only to see." Instead of "to more wisely select," write "to select more wisely." Put adverbial material outside the infinitive, where it will not split the infinitive.

25. You used an elementary encyclopedia in your Works Cited.

There are several types of sources that you should not use as sources in your Works Cited. One is the elementary encyclopedia, such as *World Book* or *Americana*. These are not respectable as research sources because you do not have to search for anything: the material is pre-searched and listed in a single place alphabetically. Furthermore, the articles in encyclopedias are written at a universal, elementary level, and only skim the surface of the subject in the briefest way. You will not learn much there, but you might get some initial ideas for real research by reading an encyclopedia article. A second source of material that you should avoid is the *Cliff's Notes* or *Monarch's Notes* sort of pre-digested analysis. These booklets are literary analysis at its lowest level and are not respected as research sources. You would be far better off to seek out important biographies and noted works of literary criticism. A final source that you must avoid is the slip, or jacket cover, blurb on a book. To quote from a slip is to suggest that you have only skimmed the surface, and did not take the time to read the book. Find advanced sources of information in the library and bookstore.

26. Avoid self-reference.

Avoid self-reference--focus on the thesis. It is important to avoid self-reference of all forms when writing a formal paper. By *self-reference* I mean referring to yourself in the first person singular (I), referring to the paper itself (In this paper I intend . . .), or even referring to quotations you have presented as quotations (This quotation means that . . .). Why should you avoid self-reference? Well, when you point to something, you want a person to look at the thing, and not at your hand. Mentioning yourself, your paper, or your quotations only breaks the reader's concentration by drawing attention away from the ideas and toward the medium. Do not break the spell; get the reader thinking about Sophocles, and keep the reader thinking about Sophocles. In other words do not unintentionally write papers about themselves or about yourself; intentionally write papers about ideas.

This does not mean that you do not include your own thinking in your paper. It only means that you present your ideas without referring to yourself in the first person. Just present the idea; you do not need to say "I think" because your name at the top of the page informs us whose views these are, if they are not documented as being the views of someone else.

27. You have an over-reliance on one source.

When most of the quotes in a research paper are from a single source, especially if they are from only a few pages of a single source or if they are presented in page-number order from a single source, this gives the reader the impression that the paper is not a research paper but a book report. For best effect, you need to present the reader with a diverse collection of research evidence, avoiding the impression that you relied too much on one or two sources.

28. Your title is not accurate.

Please write an accurate title for your paper. As I have discussed in class, the title of a formal paper should be true, precise, and specific. It should be, probably, a thumbnail expression of the thesis, rather than a mere general categorical term. A paper on imagery in *Hamlet*, therefore, should not be titled "Shakespeare," but should be "Imagery in Shakespeare's *Hamlet*." If a title is too broad, it is actually false because the paper does not really discuss what the title promises, but only a small portion of it.

29. Enclose appositives in commas.

Punctuate appositives correctly. It is good to use appositives--interrupting definitions--to insert information gracefully into sentences, especially early in a research paper when you might be mentioning names or titles unfamiliar to the reader, but remember that appositives take TWO COMMAS or none--usually two, and you must not forget the second appositive comma: Ted Hughes, Plath's former husband, wrote in praise of Plath's writings.

30. Punctuate dashes and hyphens correctly.

Please notice exactly the difference between the way dashes and hyphens are made. In professional publishing a true dash is simply a longer mark than a hyphen (It looks like this—not this-see?), but in Courier type font, a dash is a two-hyphen mark used to indicate abrupt breaks in thought--like that, whereas a hyphen is a one-stroke mark used to glue two words into one-thought units. Some manuals suggest that you make a dash with two blank spaces and only one hyphen - like that, but do not. Use two hyphens and no spaces for a dash, and one hyphen and no spaces for a hyphen, and then there is no doubt which mark you really intended. Remember the logic that a dash is a break but a hyphen is glue.

31. You use the wrong word (w or ww)

Choose your words carefully. My mark *w* means that you have used the wrong word. It is easy to use a word that sounds impressive but that has a wrong or even absurd meaning in your sentence. If, for example, you say that "Sinclair's family sided with the movements of the Confederacy," I wonder what you mean. Political movements? Military movements? In this case *movements* would seem to be the wrong word for your sentence. You could leave it out: "Sinclair's family sided with the Confederacy." Or you could change it to something more direct: "Sinclair's family sided with the states/arguments/opinions of the Confederacy." Be wary of picking words for their sound; sense comes first.

32. You have an indentation error. (5> 10>)

Indent paragraphs, long quotes, and Works Cited properly. A 5> or a 10> mark means that you should have indented the line five spaces or the quote ten spaces. In accordance with the MLA instructions, we put exactly five blank spaces at the beginning of a paragraph, and we start typing on the sixth space. We put exactly ten blank spaces before each line of a long quotation, and we start typing on the eleventh space. The second line, not the first, of each Works Cited listing should be indented five spaces. You can indent by hitting the space bar repeatedly, but it is easier to set your tabs at the fifth and tenth space.

33. Use ragged-right margin, not justified.

Use a ragged-right margin. Please do not justify the right margin of your paper. Instead, use a ragged-right margin, set approximately one inch from the right edge. Even though a justified margin is beautiful, it distorts the spacing of words within the lines, and I cannot then tell whether or not you have made spacing errors.

34. Punctuate dates correctly. (1800s)

In punctuating the names of centuries, such as the 1800s or the 1900s, do not insert an apostrophe before the *s*. For example, you should type 1700s rather than 1700's. This is correct: "During the 1970s Borges wrote fiction."

35. Follow the MLA rules for the title of your paper.

Construct your title correctly. Please review the MLA requirements for the title of the paper. The title should be exactly centered, should be double-spaced, should not be in ALL CAPS, should have the First Letter of Each Major Word-- but not prepositions or articles--Capitalized, and should not be underlined, unless you underline to indicate a book title or something else that belongs in italics. You should only double-space down to the title from the date above, and you should double-space down to the first paragraph from the title. If you use both a title and subtitle, use a colon and a blank space between them: H.G. Wells: Master of Science Fiction. If the title takes up more than one line, break the title at an appropriate mid-point, rather than have just one word or two on the second line, and double-space between the two lines of the title.

36. Punctuate the apostrophe in possessives correctly.

Learn to use possessive apostrophes correctly. We always make a noun, singular or plural, possessive by ADDING something to it. We make singular nouns possessive by adding an apostrophe and an *s*, even when the noun already ends in *s*. Thus, we would type *poetess's*, not *poetess'*; *Euripides's*, not *Euripides'*; *Dickens's*, not *Dickens'* or worse *Dicken's*; *Herodotus's*, not *Herodotus'*; and *Sophocles's*, not *Sophocles'*. If the noun is plural instead of singular, then we simply add the apostrophe: the *dogs'* houses, many *authors'* ideas. In no case would we take a plural noun such as *authors* or a proper noun such as *Socrates* and insert an apostrophe into it because the noun ends in *s*: *Socrate's*! Apostrophes should never mutilate words. We form possessives by ADDING either an apostrophe or an apostrophe and an *s*. The possessive of the proper noun *Parmenides* is *Parmenides's*, not *Parmenide's*; the sophist's name was not *Parmenide*.

Caution: Do not use apostrophes in ordinary plurals that are not possessive: "Epictetus taught that ordinary philosopher's were free" is an error because no apostrophe should be used; the word *philosophers* is an ordinary plural common noun.

By the way, some style manuals would allow you to drop the *s* after singular possessives, but I would prefer that you do not; I prefer the old-fashioned way, which is also preferred by MLA and by Strunk and White in their classic writing text, *The Elements of Style*.

37. Use correct commas in year, city, nation.

Please remember that the year, city, and nation are often used as appositives and therefore require commas before and after. Thus, we say "August 20, 1947, was hot" or "Dublin, Ireland, is damp" or "Chicago, Illinois, is busy" and we are required to put the second comma in each case. Failure to put the second comma usually warps the meaning of the sentence, because it makes the second word, rather than the first, the subject of a verb. What if someone asks where I am going, and I answer, "Chicago, Illinois is my home." That means I am going to Chicago, but my home is somewhere in Illinois. If I answer, "Chicago, Illinois, is my home," then that means Chicago is my home. To change commas is to change meanings. Put a comma before and after an appositive.

38. Put things as such in italics. (In the past these were underlined.)

Italicize when you are referring to a word itself. Please remember that words, numbers, and letters as such must be placed in italics. In this way we distinguish the word *dog* from the animal, dog. We use *b*'s in spelling, and we use *3*'s in counting. See? We also place foreign language words in italics: Homer begins his story *in medias res*, in the middle of things. This technique will be especially important when you are analyzing poetry or literature and are making reference to the words, letters, or sounds contained in the writing. Be especially sure to avoid the common mistake of putting words as such in quotation marks; we do not refer to the word "shibboleth" but to the word *shibboleth*.

39. Put no comma in parentheticals.

Do not put commas in the parenthetical documentary notes. In an MLA-style parenthetical documentary notation, we do not put a comma between the author's name and the page number. The note should look like this (Euripides 64) rather than like this (Euripides, 64).

40. Space your parenthetical notes correctly. (#)

Space correctly before parenthetical notes for long and short quotations. My # mark means that you have made a spacing error in a parenthetical documentary note. Remember that spaces are language objects, just as letters are. You have to get them right. When you use a short quotation, first give the quotation in quotation marks, and skip ONE space before the documentary note "like this" (Thompson 78). "Do not omit the space like this"(Thompson 78) or put two spaces "like this" (Thompson 78).

> On long quotations, skip TWO spaces after the period at the end
> of the quotation before you type the documentary note. It should
> look like this. (Thompson 78)

Mary Stonecraft

Mr. Godwin

English Honors

23 January 2008

Shelley's Concept of Colossal Decay

In 1817 the British poet Percy Bysshe Shelley--whose wife was Mary Shelley, the author of *Frankenstein*--agreed to a poem competition with his friend Horace Smith. Both men wrote sonnets about Ozymandias, the Greek name for the ancient Egyptian king Rameses II who lived from 1304-1237 B.C. In Shelley's sonnet a traveler who has been to Egypt reports that "two vast and trunkless legs of stone / Stand in the desert . . . near them, on the sand, / Half sunk a shattered visage lies" (2-4); it is the ruin of a colossus of Ramses II, protruding from the desert sand. On the pedestal of the broken statue an inscription that asserts almost infinite power is incised into the stone: "My name is Ozymandias, King of Kings, / Look on my works ye Mighty, and despair!" (10-11). The words are in sharp contrast to the context of destruction that surrounds them:

> My name is Ozymandias, King of Kings,
> Look on my Works ye Mighty, and despair!
> Nothing beside remains. Round the decay
> Of that colossal Wreck, boundless and bare,
> The lone and level sands stretch far away. (10-14)

that even the mighty would despair, is gone.

LOGIC AND EVIDENCE

"No one's say-so is evidence." - Carl Sagan

In a democracy each citizen has an equal right to express an opinion, but this does not mean that all opinions are equally true. Opinions can be wrong, false, even ridiculous—especially if the facts are wrong or the reasoning is bogus. In advanced academic writing, we construct a case that our thesis is not a mere personal opinion; it is the truth. This puts special burdens on us, as writers, to get our facts right and reasons straight.

At its heart your paper is about an idea: the thesis. If we consider the four steps of core element grading, we see that the purpose of the first three elements—correct English, format, and essay structure—is to deliver the fourth element: your idea. The whole purpose of an academic paper is to use these elements to communicate your idea.

For your paper to be intellectually meaningful, you must accomplish two things. First, your **thesis must have merit**; it must contribute an insight or perception that is not obvious and that everyone else does not already know. You must have something to show. You develop your idea in the research process. Read, read, read. That is why it is called *re-search*. Be patient when you research; Linus Pauling, the winner of two Nobel prizes, once said that the "best way to have a good idea is to have a lot of ideas," so the more *candidate ideas* you find, the more likely you are to find a good one.

Second, **your case for the thesis must be valid**. Being convincing is not enough because even specious (wrong) arguments can seem convincing. You must take the trouble to be right, and then you must construct a sharp, logical case that presents your evidence.

You may have a good thesis, but if your argument does not make sense, if your reasoning is wrong, if your statements are illogical, if your quotations are not relevant or effective, then you have not proved your thesis.

Now we begin to understand why essays have the parts they have: the structure of an essay is a logic-strategy. An essay is like a proof in geometry. The introduction presents the thesis to be proved, the body develops evidence and facts that prove it, and the conclusion extracts the essence of the body and gathers it to a perfect point.

Educated people love clear truth and careful thought. They love good ideas presented with care, with integrity, in a logical sequence, and with precise words—or in the case of mathematics, words and numbers. Educated minds like it when facts are discussed responsibly; they are uncomfortable with exaggeration, hyperbole, careless words, unfounded claims, loud voices, unsupported arguments. They take the word *know* seriously and do not say they *know* something that is only a guess or a preference.

We see this respect for truth and organization in many forms of knowledge and art. An English sonnet, for example, is a highly structured fourteen-line poem consisting of three quatrains and a couplet, with the logic being: **If** quatrain A, **and** quatrain B, **and** quatrain C, **then** couplet. We love sonnets because they combine poetry and logic perfectly (among other reasons). Here is Shakespeare's "Sonnet 73":

> That time of year thou mayst in me behold
> When yellow leaves, or none, or few, do hang
> Upon those boughs which shake against the cold,
> Bare ruin'd choirs where late the sweet birds sang.
> In me thou seest the twilight of such day
> As after sunset fadeth in the west,
> Which by and by black night doth take away,
> Death's second self that seals up all in rest.
> In me thou see'st the glowing of such fire
> That on the ashes of his youth doth lie,
> As the death-bed whereon it must expire,
> Consumed with that which it was nourish'd by.
>   This thou perceivest, which makes thy love more strong,
>   To love that well which thou must leave ere long.

Shakespeare's sonnet uses crystal structure to express the approaching end of the speaker's life. In the first quatrain the speaker compares himself to branches that have lost their leaves. In the second quatrain he compares himself to the dim light just after the sun has set. In the third quatrain he compares himself to the glowing embers of a fire that has lost its flame. These three comparisons lead to the emotional conclusion of the couplet. An essay is like that; it uses form to make thought clear.

THE SYLLOGISM

Another logical structure that illustrates careful thinking is the **syllogism** (συλλογισμός, syllogismos, in Greek). The syllogism is a logical proof developed by the ancient Greek philosopher Aristotle (384 b.c. - 322 b.c.) who was the pupil of Plato and the teacher of Alexander the Great. A syllogism is a three-part proof with a major premise, a related minor premise, and then a conclusion:

Major Premise:	All dogs have toes.
Minor Premise:	Boot is a dog.
Conclusion:	Boot has toes.

Notice that if the major premise or minor premise is false, the argument is specious:

Major Premise:	All dogs have wings.
Minor Premise:	Boot is a dog.
Conclusion:	Boot has wings.

You can also crash the logic if you change the sequence or relationship of terms:

Major Premise:	All dogs have toes.
Minor Premise:	Cats have toes.
Conclusion:	Cats are dogs.

The point: the syllogism is a shrill warning that you must be careful; you can say absurd things if you do not think logically about relationships between things and then reason correctly. In a formal paper you can use syllogistic reasoning to make important points; instead of putting the three parts of the syllogism in a column, you can put them in a paragraph. You will find the three parts of a syllogism in this sentence:

Poets pay close attention to the relationship between sound and meaning, and Sylvia Plath, one of the most important modern poets, did too, although she used subtle poetic devices to conceal the meticulous details of her art.

If we look at the pieces of the sentence, we find:

Major Premise:	Poets relate sounds to meaning.
Minor Premise:	Plath was a poet.
Conclusion:	Plath related sounds to meaning.

The point is not that all of your paragraphs should be secret syllogisms; that is not true. What is true is that correct logic is a requirement of advanced academic writing.

LOGICAL FALLACIES

We have seen that a misconstructed syllogism produces a conclusion that is false rather than true. There are other famous ways to utter nonsense, called *logical fallacies*. If something is fallacious, it is false. The word *fallacy* comes ultimately from the Latin verb *fallere*, to deceive. Fallacies do deceive; they contain faulty reasoning. Here are four of the most famous ones:

1. Ad Hominem

The Latin phrase *ad hominem* means to the man. An *ad hominem* fallacy happens when you say that something is true (or false) because a certain person said it. Essentially, we attack someone's character or intentions, rather than disproving their idea. A criminal might say something, but that does not make it false. A scientist might say something, but that does not prove it true. As Carl Sagan said, "No one's say-so is evidence."

The *ad hominem* error is especially important for advanced academic writing because we quote people to build a case, so we have to be careful that the sources we quote are reputable scholars and people with demonstrable knowledge and integrity, rather than amateurs, extremists, or people with dogmatic agendas that might cause them to write propaganda. In a criminal court, lawyers attempt to cast doubt on a witness's credibility in various ways. In a research paper we try to account for the *ad hominem* problem in two ways: by selecting credible sources, and by quoting from multiple sources that confirm one another, increasing the likelihood, we hope, that the source we quoted is right. If we can back up the quotations with experimental or statistical data, or with a collection of facts that support our quotations, even better.

2. Begging the Question

A proposition cannot prove itself. Another way of saying that is that you do not prove something by saying it again, even if you slightly change the words. You cannot argue that a policy will increase unemployment because it will cause joblessness to rise. That is begging the question. Begging the question is basing a conclusion on something already said in the premise, which means that the conclusion is nothing but a sneaky repetition of the premise.

In advanced academic writing we sometimes fall into this type of circular argument. If I say that a collection of poems is pessimistic because the poems have a doomed quality, I have proved nothing. All I did was just change *pessimistic* to *doomed* and repeat myself. Begging the question can be difficult to detect if the we conceal the fallacy by switching synonyms. This is an error you might fall into if you are writing too fast and do not realize you are repeating yourself, or if you get too talkative trying to fill a page.

3. Straw Man

In a straw man fallacy, we ignore the real idea and attack (or support) a misrepresentation or exaggeration of it. Instead of attacking the real thing, we attack a straw man and pretend it is the real idea. Anyone who is not paying close attention can be fooled. Straw man is a typical tactic of deception in dirty politics; it is a phony response, attacking what the opponent never said. If Senator Smith votes against a bill for the purchase of a new fighter-jet, an opponent might roar that Senator Smith is against national defense. The problem is that being against national defense is only a straw man, not the real position; Senator Smith did not say that, claim that, vote for that, or support that. Senator Smith voted against this bill because the airplane would not be delivered *for five years*; he supports a better defense bill that would provide a new fighter jet in two years. The opponent, though, will seek votes by howling that Senator Smith voted against our national defense. Is this dishonest? Yes. *Yes*. Learning logic protects us from liars.

In academic writing the straw man fallacy can be a risk, especially in certain types of papers. Let us use a literary example: what if you wrote that a novel is cynical because of facts in the author's private life? The book might have a disturbing theme, but the author's life does not prove it, either way. In this case the author's life is just a straw man, a side issue. To prove that the theme of the book is cynical, you must analyze the book. We must construct a proof by discussing the thing itself, not a straw man.

4. The *Post Hoc* Fallacy

The full Latin phrase for this fallacy is *Post hoc, ergo propter hoc:* after this, therefore because of this. We fall into the *post hoc* fallacy when we think that what comes before must be the cause of what comes after. If a winter is more severe than usual, and in the spring the plankton in the ocean begin to die, that does not mean that the cold weather caused the die-off; there may have been coincidental run-offs of fertilizer or pesticide into the sea. Causes do precede effects, but most effects in the world have multiple possible causes. If Sam sneezes, and then a bridge collapses, it is obvious that the sneeze did not collapse the bridge, but the *post hoc* fallacy is more difficult to detect when there is a close relationship between the before and the after.

In advanced academic writing we must beware of falling into the *post hoc* fallacy. In a literary paper, for example, if an author receives severe criticism for a novel and then announces that she will write no more novels, someone might infer that she retired because she was criticized. That is not a ridiculous hypothesis, but there could be many other reasons, such as serious illness, that caused the author to retire. You will need more than a clever hunch to have an academic paper; you will need facts, details, perhaps quotations from the author's diary or from friends who knew her at the time. You need to give your reader reasons to believe your inference. Many novelists are severely criticized; few stop writing novels. Serious scholars do intense research to verify that their guesses are based on facts; if you think A caused B, then dig into the literature and see if you can find evidence for a real connection.

You would enjoy reading more about famous fallacies. There are dozens of them, and reading about them has the cumulative effect of making you think twice about the arguments you make. Francis Bacon (1561-1626) developed a famous list of fallacies, that he called the Idols, and you would enjoy reading about those. For our purposes, we want to make sure that our points and facts are relevant and logical, and that the conclusions we draw from information are actually supported by that information.

56

Peter Quince

Mr. Mustardseed

English Honors

19 February 2009

The Puckish Wit of Robin Goodfellow

Puck, the "merry wanderer of the night" (2.1.43) in William

Shakespeare's comedy *A Midsummer Night's Dream*, is an elf, a prankish

trickster, who is a servant to Oberon, the king of the fairies.

Shakespeare's Puck is based on a traditional character, named *Puck*, in

English mythology (Starveling 271). It is from Puck that English received

the adjective *puckish*, meaning playfully mischievous, and we sense that

puckish spirit in Puck's first words in in Act II, scene I:

> Thou speakest aright;
>
> I am that merry wanderer of the night.
>
> I jest to Oberon and make him smile
>
> When I a fat and bean-fed horse beguile,
>
> Neighing in likeness of a filly foal;
>
> And sometimes lurk I in a gossip's bowl
>
> In very likeness of a roasted crab,
>
> And when she drinks, against her lips I bob
>
> And on her withered dewlap pour the ale. (2.1.42-50)

The impish idea of lurking "in a gossip's bowl, / In the very likeness

of a roasted crab" makes us laugh, and we know at once that Puck will be a

character to watch.

We get a feel for the bright spirit of this character by noticing that

he speaks in rhymed iambic meter. This elevated language distinguishes

Puck from, for example, Nick Bottom, whose incondite sentences have neither

rhyme nor meter:

> Methought I was--and methought I had--but man is but a patched
>
> fool if he will offer to say what methought I had. The eye of
>
> hath not heard, the ear of man hath not seen, man's hand is

Works Cited

Flute, Francis. *How the Elves Gained Control of the Forest*. Boston:
Highfellow, 2009.

Shakespeare, William. *A Midsummer Night's Dream: The Complete Text with
Analytical Commentary*. New York: Bignet, 1980.

Starveling, Robin. *The Mythical Background of Shakespeare's Characters*.
Chicago: Centerstate UP, 2003.

Advanced Writing Assignments

This section of the book contains four writing assignments, each more complex and challenging than the former. Each assignment begins with a reflection on vocabulary and grammar. This is followed by a special focus section of ten actual research paper comments emphasizing details of real student papers. Additional content is included in each assignment. The specifications of your writing assignments are presented at the end of each section.

FIRST PAPER: A PAPER ABOUT POETRY OR SHAKESPEARE

Powemm 1

Rita Powemm

Ms. Tagogue

English Honors

5 February 2009

Your thesis in not visible enough either in your introduction or in the vague title of the paper. The reader is still uncertain what the paper is about. The title is too general, and you take too long to get to the point.

President Lincoln's Ballads

Abraham Lincoln loved poetry. In 1844 as he was campaigning for Henry Clay, the thirty-five-year-old Abraham Lincoln returned to Indiana, the state where he had grown up. Lincoln had not returned to Indiana for fifteen years, but the scenes of his childhood and the sight of his mother's *tr* and sister's graves filled Lincoln with poignant feelings about his life. He sat down and wrote three poems, which Randall Jarret has described as "no *magnum opus*, but very good ballad stanzas" (Jarret 217).

mm Recalling his past, the first poem, "My Childhood's Home," contains ten ballad stanzas, with the first announcing the theme of sad memories:

> My childhood's home I see again,
>
> And sadden with the view;
>
> And still, as memory crowds my brain,
>
> There's pleasure in it too. (1-4)

You handle quotations well.

The memories sadden, even as they contain pleasure, but we learn more about the nature of this pleasure later in the poem. In the fifth stanza Lincoln explains that "memory will hallow all / We've known, but know no more" (5-6). Nineteen years later, Lincoln would use the word *hallow* in his Gettysburg Address, but here Lincoln feels that his memory has hallowed those things which are now lost in the past. In *The Literary Path to Gettysburg*, Scott Ridley explains clearly that:

> Lincoln was a neophyte but he had a firm grasp of poetic
>
> technique. In "My Childhood's Home" Lincoln emphasized the
>
> word *hallow* by enclosing it in words that echoed the *l*'s: "will
>
> hallow all." We see the same technique in his emphasis on soft
>
> consonants *n* and *m* in the following line. (Ridley 74)

This is an excellent quote. Is this the right place for it?

Ridley shows that Lincoln reserved the word *hallow* for occasions of maximum importance, such as the consecration of the Gettysburg battlefield,

Use Academic Words.

If you want to be a good academic writer, you will have to build a strong academic vocabulary because the casual, informal words and contractions of daily life cannot be used in a formal paper; formal papers are *formal*. Not all academic words are big words, and academic sentences are not stuffed full of big words, but there is a striking difference between ordinary language and the calm, educated, formal words of academic writing.

In Volume One of *Advanced Academic Writing*, we looked at forty words, ten per assignment, taken from Volume One of *The Word Within the Word*. Two words were chosen from each lesson of that text, and they were chosen because they were good, all-purpose academic words that might be useful in a variety of papers. It is worth the trouble to look once more at that vocabulary before we introduce the new words for this book.

It is not the number of words that we focus on now; it is the nature of the words; it the formal sound, the mostly Latin sound, the crispness of them. In this language, a false argument is *specious*, and a beginner is a *neophyte*. Too much talk is *superfluous*, and overstatement is just *hyperbole*. Little by little, you begin to hear what academic writing sounds like, beginning with the words themselves. Here again, then, are the forty words we saw in Volume One; each listing begins with the chapter of *The Word Within the Word*, Volume One, in which it appears.

	Word	Definition	Part of Speech	Example
1.	**superfluous**	excess	adjective	The objection was **superfluous**.
1.	**posthumously**	after death	adverb	The book was published **posthumously**.
2.	**neophyte**	beginner	noun	As a poet, he was a **neophyte**.
2.	**incredulous**	disbelieving	adjective	The readers were **incredulous**.
3.	**specious**	false	adjective	The **specious** argument convinced him.
3.	**elucidate**	explain	verb	Harper Lee **elucidated** the scene.
4.	**equanimity**	calmness	noun	Ahab's **equanimity** was startling.
4.	**magnum opus**	great work	noun	*Walden* was Thoreau's **magnum opus**.
5.	**hyperbole**	overstatement	noun	The claim was mere **hyperbole**.
5.	**altruism**	selflessness	noun	Toad was not known for **altruism**.

In the first ten, the superstars are *specious*, *elucidate*, *hyperbole*, and *superfluous*. Each of these words is strongly academic and formal in tone, and each one is extremely common in academic contexts. Something is *specious* when it is deceptively appealing but false. In his magnum opus, *The Decline and Fall of the Roman Empire*, Edward Gibbon used *specious* repeatedly. To *elucidate* is to explain, to cast light on a subject. *Hyperbole* is exaggeration for effect; it is not intended to deceive or to be taken literally. *Superfluous* means too much, more than is required; there can be superfluous cash or superfluous chatter.

6. **egregious**	shocking	adjective	It was an **egregious** offense.
6. **preclude**	prevent	verb	His statement **precluded** any resolution.
7. **egocentric**	self-centered	adjective	It is **egocentric** poetry.
7. **exculpate**	exonerate	verb	Her alibi **exculpated** her from blame.
8. **supersede**	replace	verb	The new rule **superseded** all others.
8. **vociferous**	loud	adjective	Long John was a **vociferous** villain.
9. **platitude**	a trite remark	noun	The essay is full of hollow **platitudes**.
9. **colloquial**	conversational	adjective	The text was **colloquial**, not formal.
10. **discursive**	rambling	adjective	The essay was **discursive**, unfocused.
10. **pedestrian**	inferior	adjective	We soon tired of his **pedestrian** babble.

In the second ten, pay particular attention to *supersede*, which means to replace all that have come before; we might say that a new form of analysis supersedes the one currently is use. *Preclude* is another word in frequent use; to preclude is to prevent something in advance, before it even has time to happen; precluding something makes it impossible. The death of a Roman senator precluded the emperor's planned persecution of him.

11. **prolific**	productive	adjective	Dickinson was a **prolific** poet.
11. **soporific**	sleep-inducing	adjective	The **soporific** speech put us to sleep.
12. **idiosyncrasy**	peculiarity	noun	The mannerism was an **idiosyncrasy**.
12. **bon mot**	witticism	noun	Oscar Wilde uttered a classic **bon mot**.
13. **penultimate**	next to last	adjective	His **penultimate** novel was a failure.
13. **vacuous**	stupid	adjective	His comments were **vacuous**.
14. **malevolent**	malicious	adjective	Boo was a **malevolent** phantom.
14. **disclose**	reveal	verb	Plath did not **disclose** her meaning.
15. **indolent**	lazy	adjective	Like other **indolent** writers, he failed.
15. **effulgence**	radiance	noun	They lauded him with effulgent praise.

In the third group we see powerful words such as *prolific*, which means producing something in abundance. There are prolific novelists and poets, for example, who produce work after work. Another power word is *vacuous*, a term of derision; it means that something is so stupid that it is a vacuum. Many historical figures have idiosyncrasies; an *idiosyncrasy* is a peculiarity, such as the Confederate general Stonewall Jackson's idiosyncrasy of continually sucking lemons. Notice that the spelling is *idiosyncrasy*, not *indiosyncracy*.

16.	**anthology**	collection	noun	We read an **anthology** of poetry.
16.	**incoherent**	confusing	adjective	The paper was completely **incoherent**.
17.	**commensurate**	in proportion	adjective	The pay is **commensurate** with the job.
17.	**acrimony**	bitterness	noun	He felt no **acrimony** towards Coleridge.
18.	**ossify**	turn to bone	verb	His ideas had **ossified** into inflexibility.
18.	**xenophobic**	afraid of foreigners	adjective	The book was a **xenophobic** diatribe.
19.	**pathos**	pity	noun	The story evoked tragic **pathos**.
19.	**gravamen**	essence	noun	I understood the **gravamen** of her story.
20.	**delineate**	to outline	verb	He quickly **delineated** the plan.
20.	**melancholy**	deep sadness	noun	Werther descended into **melancholy**.

The fourth group contains the power word *incoherent*; something that is incoherent does not cohere; it does not stick together. If your essay is incoherent, that means that it is just a bunch of broken, separate pieces, which you have not woven together into a single coherent theme. *Acrimony* is an academic word for bitterness; some presidential debates have become acrimonious. Finally, *delineate* means to outline precisely; it can refer to geography, as when two countries hold talks to delineate the border between them. If you never delineate your thesis sharply enough in your paper, that is a serious problem.

As you begin to build your collection of academic words and your sense of their grammatical use, remember not to overuse them. Great writers do not overload sentences with big words. You will use these words if they are right for your sentence, not just to sound impressive. Notice: this is the fourth sentence in this paragraph, and even though this paragraph has no big academic words in it, it is still completely academic in its vocabulary and tone.

Discussion Question:
In each of the four groups, select one word that I did not discuss, but that you think is likely to be important. Explain why you think it is important.

Now let us look at new vocabulary, this time from *The Word Within the Word*, Volume Two. As we did in Volume One, we will study ten academic words per assignment. The numbers at left are the chapter numbers of *Word Within the Word*, Volume Two.

	Word	Definition	Part of Speech	Example
31.	**hierarchy**	ranking	noun	There was a **hierarchy** of values.
31.	**nonplussed**	perplexed	adjective	He was **nonplussed** by the question.
32.	**putative**	thought-to-be	adjective	He was the **putative** head of the mafia.
32.	**alter ego**	second self	noun	Horatio was Hamlet's **alter ego**.
33.	**impugn**	attack as false	verb	The critic **impugned** his motives.
33.	**fortissimo**	loudly	adv. or adj.	The **fortissimo** passage woke him.
34.	**sedate**	calm	adjective	The **sedate** prose lulled us.
34.	**retort**	swift reply	noun	Hamlet's **retort** stunned Polonius.
35.	**reify**	treat as real	verb	The abstraction had been **reified**.
35.	**anthropocentric**	man-centered	adjective	The myths were **anthropocentric**.

In this list we see *putative*, pronounced PYOO-ta-tive. Something is putative if it is generally thought to be so; Aristotle, for example, is the putative father of formal logic, and Walt Whitman is the putative creator of modern free verse poetry. We might say that Nathaniel Hawthorne was Herman Melville's putative main influence when Melville was writing *Moby Dick*. *Impugn* is another strong word; it is a verb meaning to challenge or call into question, to attack as false. We might say that Senator Edward Everett privately impugned Abraham Lincoln's character and ability until he heard Lincoln give the Gettysburg Address; then, Everett became an admirer of Lincoln. The adjective *nonplussed* is powerful; it refers to the type of perplexity that results when you are both surprised and confused, leaving you uncertain how to react. In Ibsen's brilliant play, *An Enemy of the People*, Dr. Stockman is continually nonplussed because he naively expects to be hailed as a hero, even as his society scorns and rejects him.

To build a strong vocabulary, you cannot just force yourself through a regimen of flash cards. You have to think about words so deeply that you develop a love of words. If your love of words is only limited, your vocabulary will be only limited. If, on the other hand, you get a taste for the sound and power of words, your ability will grow. In the end it will be your reading, more than any vocabulary program, that will build up your vocabulary; read everything, fiction and non-fiction. Read more than any school could possibly assign to you.

Write Grammatically Correct Sentences

Academic writers do not write obliviously, unaware of the construction of their sentences. Instead, there is a grammatical self-awareness that is one of the best pleasures of writing. With grammar you know—as you write it—that the sentence is correct, and you enjoy seeing the pieces snap into correct places. This example is from *4Practice, Volume Two*:

From Jane Austen's *Pride and Prejudice*, 1813

	When	he	spoke,	his	accent	had	none	of	its	usual	**sedateness**.
Parts of Speech	conj.	pron.	v.	adj.	n.	v.	pron.	prep.	adj.	adj.	n..
Parts of Sentence		subj.	AVP		subj.	AVP	D.O.				
Phrases								----------------prep. phr.--------------			
Clauses	------dependent clause------			--------------------------independent clause----------------------------							
				a D,I complex declarative sentence							

Grammar: Here is a classic D,I complex sentence, beginning with a subordinating conjunction *when* that introduces the dependent clause. The possessive adjective *its* does not have an apostrophe, nor should it have one.

Vocabulary: To be sedate is to be calm, dignified, unhurried, perhaps boring; *sed* means sit. The adjective *sedate* was derived from the noun *sedation*. W34 (W34 means that the word comes from *The Word Within the Word*, Volume Two, List 34).

Poetics: Notice the *s* sounds in this sentence: *Spoke hiS aCCent itS SedatneSS*. The sentence has a lovely rhythm.

Writing: In this sentence structure is truth; the big idea is the independent clause, for which the dependent clause gives background. The independent clause flows to a crescendo in its finale, *sedateness*, full of elegant connotation.

Punctuation: The D,I comma after the introductory dependent clause is required.

Actual Research Paper Comments

In the first section of this book I reviewed and discussed the forty actual research paper comments that appeared in Volume One of this series. You are now assumed to understand and to be able to apply those forty ideas and to be eager for forty more. This process must be cumulative; we cannot leave knowledge behind, darkening in the past.

Let us now look at ten more actual research paper comments. Keep in mind that these are real comments that were developed as responses to real student papers. We will have seen some of these ideas in other discussions, and we will visit them again; the point here is that these comments are collected from years of grading real papers; they are comments, both negative and positive, that benefit most students:

```
1. You analyze your quotations well.
I like the way you take the time to discuss your quotations after you present
them, calling attention to the details that you find significant.  Continue to
develop that; it is a good technique for communicating your most important ideas
clearly.
```

```
2. You use appositives well.
I appreciate the way you use appositives to identify the sources of your
quotations.  On the one hand, it is disconcerting to continually see the
names of experts unknown to us, and on the other hand, it is informative and
clarifying to be told that an expert being cited is a scholar in a certain field
and is the author of a specific title on the subject.  You have done a good job
of informing your reader who your sources are.  Remember that an appositive must
be enclosed in two commas:  Jacques Cousteau, the inventor of the aqua-lung,
arrived in Madrid.
```

```
3. Your paragraphs must be real. (¶)
Group your sentences into real paragraphs.  The paragraph symbol ¶ indicates
the location of paragraph problems in your paper.  In organized, advanced
thinking, such as an essay, you cannot let your ideas wander randomly.  The
ideas have to be grouped into a simple, comprehensible structure that someone,
including you yourself, can understand.  Sentences have to be separated into
clear paragraphs.  A paragraph is a group of sentences all about ONE THING.
All of the sentences might describe an event in time order.  They might explain
a thought in logical order.  They might present a conclusion by proceeding
from concrete to abstract.  But the sentences of a paragraph must be ordered,
and they must belong together in the same place, like the sentences in this
paragraph I am writing now.  In other words, if you indent, you are telling
the reader that all sentences between here and the next indent are about the
```

same thing, so this must be the TRUTH. If you are discussing the theme of man versus woman in Sophocles's *Antigone* in a paragraph, then you may not include the conflict between the brothers Eteocles and Polyneices in the same paragraph, because that conflict is not about man versus woman. Separate your sentences into the paragraphs in which they belong.

4. Your essay does not focus on the thesis. Use a microlanguage.
I think that the thesis of this paper is not focused enough or easy enough to follow. I had to look back over the paper after I finished reading it in order to remember and retrace the ideas. Remember that a thesis essay must be a self-focusing design: you must construct it so that it is clearly focused on the thesis; the reader must not be given the task of figuring out how things are related to each other; that is your creative challenge. One of the best ways to do this is to use key thesis language, what I would call a *microlanguage*: several key thesis words that you introduce in the title and introduction and then continually repeat throughout the paper. If your thesis is that Euripides was a *philanthropic pacifist*, then you would explicitly express the ideas of the paragraphs in terms of how they demonstrate that Euripides was *philanthropic* or how he was a *pacifist*. Those two words would keep reappearing, tying the whole paper together. Every paragraph should have such a thread that is tied to the central thesis. Finish by using these same words in your conclusion.

5. Your thesis should be challenging.
Have an intellectually challenging thesis. One of the marks of a strong essay is that it has a challenge factor; it is worth reading because it asserts a point of view that needs proving, one that many readers would doubt. Merely to write a paper offering a summary of a plot, or a noncontroversial glimpse of someone's poetry, or a polite review of someone's novel, or a hands-off explanation of an well-accepted theory, is to bore and disappoint the reader, asking him to bear with you for little apparent reason. You are proving something no one doubts! The reason a strong thesis is enlightening is that it surprises us, it changes our mind, it proves to us that we had it wrong, it leaves us with a new perspective. It is this ability of a strong thesis to challenge and enlighten us that is the mark of a best paper.

6. Make lists and compounds parallel. (//)
Keep lists and compounds grammatically parallel. My mark // means that you have a parallelism error. Lists and compounds need to be written in parallel form. You could list adjective, adjective, and adjective. Or you could list noun, noun, and noun. But you should not list noun, noun, and adjective. You might list three prepositional phrases: of the people, by the people, and for the people. If you use a preposition in the first item, use it throughout. If you use the same preposition twice in a list, then use it the third time also: "Socrates is mentioned in Plato's Dialogues, in Aristotle's works, and in Xenophon's works." Compounds should be treated the same way; the compounded elements in compound subjects, direct objects, or subject complements should be

parallel in grammar. It would be wrong to say, "I like to think and swimming." Make it parallel: "I like to think and to swim." Use two infinitives, or use two gerunds, but don't compound an infinitive with a gerund. You must also use parallelism when you use the correlative conjunctions: We seek not only TO be more virtuous, but also TO fulfill our hopes of happiness. If you use an infinitive on the left side, then use an infinitive on the right side also.

7. Do not make pronoun reference errors. (ref)

Make sure your pronoun references are clear. My *ref* mark means that you have made a pronoun reference error. Remember that pronouns are designed to be universal, and that therefore you must take pains to insure that their references to specific nouns are clear. Always ask yourself, he who?, she who? his who?, our who? who are they?, what is it? Especially when you have mentioned several different persons, the use of personal pronouns is risky, because there might be antecedent ambiguity as to which of the persons is indicated by the pronoun: "Epictetus spoke of people who expressed conceit towards others, but in doing so they lost self-control." Which they? It is also easy to make a missing antecedent reference error in which you use *it* or *this* before you have even mentioned anything *it* or *this* could refer to! In fact, I recommend that you never use *this* as the subject of a sentence; only use it to modify a noun subject: "This style made Dickens famous." Is that not better than "This made Dickens famous"? Another beginner's reference error is the talking document: "in that essay it talks about" or "in this discussion it says"; essays do not talk, authors do. Use a proper noun author's name in place of the third person singular neuter gender pronoun it: "In his essay, Octavio Paz argues . . .."

8. Your proofreading is inadequate.

Your proofreading is only partly effective. Even though your paper is largely free of irritating elementary errors, you have still allowed a few (that is too many) to slip through. Yes, few is better than many, but the principle is that in an advanced class no elementary error is acceptable. Please work harder on proofreading.

9. Do not create sentence fragments in your quotes. (frag)

Avoid creating sentence fragments in quotations. When you alter a quotation by using an ellipsis . . . to indicate where you have omitted words you did not need or by inserting words that you enclose in [brackets], be sure that you do so in a way that allows the quotation to read naturally and logically, at least when it is connected to your own words that precede or follow it. Make sure that the thought is still complete and not just a sentence fragment. In other words, do not chop the quotation up so that it makes no sense or so that the reader has to reread the quotation to see why it makes sense.

10. Have a balance between your own words and quotations.

Create a balance between quotations and your own words. One thing you need to develop is a more even balance between the amount of your own writing and the amount of quotation you present. An over-reliance on either is a problem. If there are too many quotations and not enough of your own writing, then you become too invisible; the reader cannot tell who you are or what you think. The main structure of the paper must be written by you and express your ideas. The paper, in other words, should not be a chain of quotes. On the other hand, if the whole paper is in your own words with few quotations presented as evidence, then the reader will feel that you have not presented enough researched evidence to make your thesis convincing. You need the quotes for the proof. The reader will doubt your ideas if you seem unable to support them. You must construct a careful balance between your own writing and quotations so that the reader sees the thoughts of your mind, supported by the thoughts of other minds.

Do not just skim these comments or read them once in passing; study them closely, patiently, and then read them again. Discuss them. Do what you must to internalize them permanently, so that you can always apply them when you are writing academic language.

Discussion Question:
Of the ten comments, select the two that you think will improve your own writing most. Explain why you picked those two.

94

Rita,

I thoroughly enjoyed your interesting paper on Sylvia Plath's poem "The Moon and the Yew Tree." Your paper is written in good English, the MLA format is almost perfect, the essay form is clear and well-designed, and your insights into the meaning of Plath's poem are impressive. I especially enjoyed your analysis of the vowels and consonants in the lines "Fumy, spiritous mists inhabit this place, / Separated from my house by a row of headstones." Congratulations on a fine paper; this is advanced academic writing. There are, of course, some details that you missed and a few elements that you need to improve, but this is a fine paper. Let us look at a few details that still need work.

On page 2. Do not create sentence fragments in your quotes. (frag) Avoid creating sentence fragments in quotations. When you alter a quotation by using an ellipsis . . . to indicate where you have omitted words you did not need or by inserting words that you [brackets] be

Writing about Poetry

Would you be surprised if I told you that papers about poetry are among the most important you will ever write? Perhaps you would, but it is true. You will likely have to write many academic papers about poetry, and that is a good thing. It is easy to misunderstand and underestimate both the nature and the intellectual importance of poetry. Not only are great poems among the most famous and profound works of art in western civilization, but the study of poetry has been the training ground for great prose writers, not just for poets. Most great novelists also wrote poems and used those poetry techniques in the prose sentences of their novels; if we miss the poetics of their prose, we are missing something important. If you want to study formal poetics, my poetry text that accompanies this book is *Poetry, Plato, and the Concept of Beauty*, published by Royal Fireworks Press.

Because poems are often less than one page in length, and because they are set up differently on the page than ordinary paragraphs are, questions arise about how to discuss, quote, and document poems. Let us look at some of the standards.

Titles in quotation marks. Titles of short poems are in quotation marks, not italics.

Line numbers, not page numbers. In citing poems we do not put page numbers in the parenthetical documentation; instead, we give line numbers.

Quoting four lines or more. If you quote four lines or more of a poem, you must block indent the passage ten spaces. If the poem has creative spacing as part of its appearance, try to reproduce the spacing of the original poem. If you omit an entire line or more from the middle of the quotation, put one line of ellipses to indicate the missing lines.

Quoting three lines or fewer. If you quote three lines or fewer from a poem, then you do not need to indent ten spaces. Enclose the quotation in quotation marks, and use slashes with spaces on each side to indicate line endings.

Study these techniques on the following page.

Abbey Rowed

Mr. Retour

English Honors

13 April 2009

The Monstrous Crying of Wind

    In 1916 the Irish poet William Butler Yeats wrote "To a Child Dancing in the Wind," one of the poems that established his reputation as "one of the foremost poets of the twentieth century" (Martin 64). The poem contains only twelve lines in three quatrains, with rhyme scheme ababcdcdefef. The poem provides a sharp contrast between an old man who knows the tragedies of life and a young child--we do not know whether the child is a boy or girl--who is joyfully unaware of the despair and loss that life can contain. The narrator speaks to the child, though the words are an internal commentary that the child cannot hear:

> DANCE there upon the shore;
>
> What need have you to care
>
> For wind or water's roar?
>
> And tumble out your hair
>
> That the salt drops have wet; (1-5)

    Yeats uses three kinds of sentences to organize the poem. The first sentence is imperative, a command, and it communicates an incredulity that the child can be dancing and not hear the "wind or water's roar" (3). The roaring wind of tragedy is the image that dominates the poem; we see *wind* in the title, in line three, and as the final word of the poem.

    The second section of the poem is declarative, rather than imperative. The narrator reflects that "Being young you have not known / The fool's triumph, nor yet / Love lost as soon as won" (6-8). The shock that a fool could win is conveyed by a change of meter; most of the poem is iambic trimeter, but the word *triumph*, a trochee with the first syllable stressed, reverses and disrupts the rhythm, illuminating the victorious fool.

    The final section of the poem is interrogative; the narrator asks "What need have you to dread / The monstrous crying of wind!" (11-12). In these

Works Cited: Review, Poems, and Verse Plays

Every MLA paper ends in a Works Cited page that provides information about the books, journals, and other works that are cited in the paper. We always give proper credit to the authors we cite, not only because it is plagiarism not to, but because it is an intellectual pleasure to participate in a tradition of honor and integrity that has existed for centuries. It is *fun* to pay respect, with a citation, to an author who wrote a wonderful passage or who did brilliant research. We become honorable by paying honor to others.

Here is how the documentation works. For ordinary quotations, we follow each quotation with a parenthetical note containing the author's last name and the page number of the book where we found the words. There is *no comma* between these two items: (Cummings 231). This lets the reader turn to the Works Cited page, scan down the alphabetized names to *Cummings*, and find the book, its title, city of publication, publisher, and date of publication.

If, however, we are quoting a poem, we often simply provide line numbers rather than author and page number, and it looks like this, if we are citing lines four through nine: (4-9). This lets the reader find the poem in *any* book and go directly to the lines in question. We will still list the book we used in our Works Cited, as we will see below.

Like the rest of the paper, the Works Cited page is double-spaced and has a one-inch margin all around, with the header one-half inch down from the top. The listings are flush left in their first lines, but indented five spaces afterwards—the opposite of the way we treat paragraphs. The simplest listing is a **book by one author**, like this:

1. Author's last name.
2. Comma and one space.
3. Author's first name.
4. Period and two spaces.
5. Book title in *italics*.
6. Period, two spaces.
7. City of publication.
8. Colon and one space.
9. Publisher, abbreviated.
10. Comma, and one space.
11. Date of publication.
12. Period.

Murphy, Mary. *My War in the Pacific*. Chicago: Bibliobooks, 2001.

Do not write out the full name of the publisher, only its abbreviation. The *MLA Handbook* provides a long list of publisher abbreviations: *Random House* is just *Random*, *Penguin Books* is *Penguin*, *University of Chicago Press* is just *U of Chicago P*, and *Harvard University Press* is just *Harvard UP*.

A book by multiple authors.

When you cite a book by multiple authors, list them in the same order as they appear in the title page of the book, and give first name first after the first author.

```
                                                  Johnson 4
                        Works Cited
     Jones, Mark, and Robert Adams.  Thirteen Ways of Looking at Wallace
          Stevens's Poetry.  Chicago: Bartrum, 2001.
```

Multiple books by the same author.

If you use more than one book by the same author, do not list out the full name each time. Alphabetize the listings by the same author by their titles, and instead of retyping the author's name each time, type three hyphens.

```
                                                  Johnson 4
                       Works Cited
     Hargrave, Michelle.  Emerson, Poe, and the Politics of Poetics.  New
          York: Bignet, 2007.
     ---.  Thomas Hardy and His Critics: A Story of Literary Discouragement.
          Des Moines: Randle, 2002.
     ---.  Xenophon and the Anabasis.  Chicago: U of Martin P, 1998.
```

An Introduction (or Preface or Foreword).

Often, you can find outstanding commentary in the introduction to a classic novel; typically, the introduction is written by a specialist in the literature, or by a specialist on that particular author. If you wish to quote from an introduction, list it by the name of the person who wrote the introduction:

```
                                                  Johnson 4
                      Works Cited
     Gregson, Susan.  Introduction.  Treasure Island.  By Robert Louis Stevenson.
          Chicago: Bartrum, 2001.
     Riddle, George.  Foreword.  Great Expectations.  By Charles Dickens.  New
          York: Randle, 1992.
```

An Article in a Periodical

Periodicals are journals that appear periodically, at regular intervals. Such a journal might appear quarterly and have five or six articles devoted to a particular field of study. If you wish to cite a periodical, use the author's name first, the title of the article in quotation marks, the title of the journal in italics, the volume number, date, and the page numbers of the article. Punctuate and space it this way:

```
                                                     Johnson 4
                        Works Cited
     Gregson, Susan.  "The Odyssey of Jim Hawkins."  The Stevenson Quarterly
          Review.  2 (2008): 27-32.
```

A Poem in an Anthology

What if you only quote from one poem in an anthology? We know that you will usually provide only line numbers, rather than author and page number, in your parenthetical documentation. How do you list the book in your Works Cited? By poet? By the editor of the anthology? You list the poem by the poet, then give the title of the poem, the title of the book in italics, then the editor's name preceded by the abbreviation *Ed.*, then city, publisher, year and page numbers. It looks like this:

```
                                                     Johnson 4
                        Works Cited
     Yeats, William.  "To a Child Dancing in the Wind."  An Anthology of Irish
          Poetry.  Ed. William Cuhulain.  Dublin: Greenbrae, 2001.  37-38.
```

Poetry from a Verse Play such as Shakespeare

If you are citing a passage from a verse play, such as Shakespeare's *Romeo and Juliet*, you do not use the usual pattern of author and page number in your parenthetical. Instead, you give act, scene, and line number, so it looks like this, if you are quoting from act two, scene one, lines 39-45: (2.1.39-45). This way, the reader can find the quote in any copy of the play. The Works Cited listing looks like this, if you are using a typical paperback book containing only one play:

```
                                                     Johnson 4
                        Works Cited
     Shakespeare, William.  Hamlet.  New York: Randall, 2007.
```

Donald Bain

Mrs. Graymalkin

English Honors

17 March 2008

The Influence of Shakespeare on Sylvia Plath

Sylvia Plath's second book of poems, *Ariel*, was published in 1965, two years after her death. The book did much to establish Plath's reputation as a leading modern poet. Leonard Paddock, professor of literature at Heath University, has said that "Plath's fame as a poet would be different if not for the *Ariel* poems, which rise at times to a Shakespearean level of power" (Paddock 87).

Paddock's comment suggests an interesting question: in what sense did Plath's poetic technique derive directly from Shakespeare? Did she knowingly employ strategies that she had seen in Shakespeare? A series of five line-by-line comparisons does provide some evidence that Shakespeare was a model for Plath.

One of Plath's possible influences was Shakespeare's tragedy *Macbeth*. Among Shakespeare's most powerful poetry is Act One, scene one, in *Macbeth*, where the three witches send their fiendish chant into the shifting mist: "Fair is foul, and foul is fair, / Hover through the fog and filthy air" (1.1.12-13). In this passage we hear the hiss of the air in the *f*, *h*, *v*, and *th* consonants of *fair*, *foul*, *hover*, *through*, *fog*, *filthy*, and *air*. The accumulation of breathy sounds creates a sense of insidious menace. We can compare these lines to similar lines from Plath's poem, "The Moon and the Yew Tree." Describing the "light of the mind," which is "cold and planetary" (1), Plath says that "Fumy, spiritous mists inhabit this place" (5). As we saw in Shakespeare's *Macbeth*, Plath uses the hissing consonants *f*, *h*, and *th*, as well as *s*, to convey the toxic evil of the environment. As an environment of dangerous, overwhelming sounds, it is very reminiscent of Shakeapeare.

that offers a suggestion of Shakespeare's influence on

Works Cited

Hewes, Ted. *I Knew Sylvia Plath, and You Are No Sylvia Plath*. New York: Halfcourt, 2003.

Paddock, Leonard. Introduction. *No Straight and Narrow Plath*. By Simon Crowell. Los Angeles: Heath UP, 2002.

Plath, Sylvia. "The Moon and the Yew Tree." *An Anthology of Modern Poetry*. Ed. Malcolm Kingson. New York: Noman, 2007.

Shakespeare, William. *Macbeth*. New York: Ramble ...

Proofreading Practice

Let us return to the problem of proofreading. Of all the steps involved in writing a formal academic paper, the most difficult to grasp may be proofreading. There is a proclivity to relax in relief once you finish your first draft, and to assume that all is well. There is a tendency for new writers to underestimate the fiendish way errors have of hiding, particularly from their authors. We imagine, when we first write academic papers, that proofreading is a sort of quick scan; it will only take a few minutes.

Wrong. Many a student has failed a major paper because he or she had a beginner's idea about what proofreading is.

Proofreading is not a quick, concluding activity. It takes time and commitment, first, because you as the writer will be partially blind to your own errors. In writer's blindness, you know what you mean, and you tend to see what you mean, rather than what you have actually typed. As the writer you can look straight at an error and not notice it. Part of becoming an excellent proofreader is rerouting your brain so that your errors become visible; so that you can look coldly at the words on the paper. Proofreading your own words is harder than proofreading someone else's.

Second, proofreading is a multi-level, complex problem. You have to proofread the grammar of every sentence. You have to proofread the punctuation of every sentence. You have to proofread the style and the choice of words. You have to proofread the essay structure and make sure that all of the paragraphs are in the correct sequence with connecting language that bridges from one paragraph to the next. You have to proofread your logic, the relevance of your quotations, the sufficiency of your proof. You have to proofread every detail of your MLA format.

This takes time, and it takes more than one pass. Proofreading a formal paper is not a ten-minute sweep. It may take four long sessions. The best students become ultra-intense about proofreading. They get those fierce, academic eyes.

Can you find fifteen errors on the opposite page? A caution: all hyphens in the long quote are correct.

Grahame, 1

Eppie Grahame

Ms. Kreeant

English Honors

17 October 2008

The False Gloom of A.E. Housman

In 1896 when Alfred Edward Housman was only thirty-seven years old he wrote "The Time You Won Your Town the Race," a poem that helped to establish his reputation as a poetic genius capable of expressing a dark spirit of resignation about Life's inexorable tragedies. The poem, together with other Houseman poems that express the same fatalistic theme, can be viewed in part through isolation and emptiness in Housman's life, but there are reasons to think that the shadows in his famous poems donot fully represent his view of life, which may have been more sedate.

"The Time You Won Your Town the Race", set at the graveside of a young athlete who has died, contain seven quatrains of iambic tetrameter with an aabb endrhyme scheme. It takes Housman only two quatrains to create both a vision of the event and a spirit of melancholy:

> The time you won your town the race
> We chaired you through the market-place;
> Man and boy stood cheering by,
> And home we brought you shoulder-high.
> To-day, the road all runners come,
> Shoulder-high we bring you home,
> and set you at your threshold down,
> Townsman of a stiller town. (1-8)

The two quattrains depict different times, with the first depicting the joyful day of athletic victory in the past and the second depicting the sad present--the day of the young athletes' burial. The two images are unified by the crowd, which in each case but for opposite reasons is bearing the boy "shoulder-high." Once "cheering" the young athlete, Housman shows the crowd as "stiller" now. The road of the race has evolved into the metaphorical road and Housman takes us to a higher level.

Grahame 4

Works Cited

Adams, Mark, and Jonas Hermanos. *British Poetry before the Turn of the Century*. New York. Halfcourt, 2005.

Black, Sol M. Introduction. *The Subtle Poetry of A.E. Housman*. By C.D. Rohm. San Francisco: Bay Area UP, 2005.

---. *A selection of*

Five Steps for Planning and Preparing Your Paper

I discussed these five steps in Volume One, but we cannot move into the first research paper of Volume Two without looking at these steps again. Here they are, revised and expanded:

1. Read, reread, take notes, type quotes, think. Incubate. Repeat as necessary.

Consider this question: what is academic writing about? How do you collect the content that you will display in an academic paper? The answer is that academic writing is about academic *reading*. Research papers are often, in essence, advanced book reports. Students who are new to this process sometimes wish to race through or even skip the reading process that builds the basis for writing, but they find out, sooner or later, that their impatience is misguided. The only result of avoiding the reading, exploring, searching and REsearching through books and journals will be to put you closer to the paper's due date, with nothing to say. Going too fast takes longer. Books are the sources for what you write, even though you create your own thesis.

Furthermore, **the focus is on books—real books, not websites**. In a typical website about, for example, the Nobel Prize-winning novelist Toni Morrison, you might see one page of information, without any indication of who wrote the page. A biography of Morrison, on the other hand, might run to three hundred pages, giving you vastly more information about her. An article in a scholarly journal might be twenty or thirty pages long. The introduction to one of her novels might be ten pages long. These are real, respectable sources. Learn to haunt the library; become familiar with nonfiction books and scholarly journals. When your college professor assigns you a term paper with five or more sources, she does not mean five one-page websites.

Another detail: **basic encyclopedias are not scholarly sources**. They are not grown-up research; they are alphabetized, pre-searched summaries. Do not quote from them or list them in your Works Cited. If you want to consult an elementary encyclopedia to get your bearings, or to get ideas for research, that is fine. We also rarely quote dictionaries, and we never quote the blurb on a book jacket because that suggests that we only read the cover of the book. There are advanced, scholarly encyclopedias, usually devoted to specific topics, and they may be used.

Step one takes time. It takes as long as it takes. Your final paper will be no better than your patience at this point. This is closely related to your enjoyment; if you adopt the mature approach of eagerly wanting to know about your subject, it is much easier to be patient and to concentrate. I like to read and research with my laptop before me, so that I can take notes and type out quotations on the spot, being sure to type a Works Cited listing for every book I use. Being slow, positive, and careful at this stage makes the other four stages easier.

Slowly, out of this reading, note-taking, and thinking, you will find possible ideas for a thesis. In your reading you will find some incredible fact to explore, or you will suddenly wonder about an interesting question, and have an idea what the answer might be. As the Nobel Prize winner Linus Pauling once said, the more ideas you have, the more likely you are to have a good idea. Do not panic if you do not know your thesis on the first day or two. Learn to work in *academic time*. Read, adjust, incubate. Think. Your thesis will slowly rise out of the books you read.

2. Organize and Outline.

Do not attempt to start writing without a plan. Your teacher may or may not require you to turn in a formal outline. For short papers such as the ones we will write, a formal outline is usually not expected. Furthermore, the imperative to learn the intricacies of outlining are different now that computer word processors have built-in outline processors. Even though teachers and professors may not ask you to turn an outline in, you can use the computer's built-in outline processor to plan your paper. That way, you know what you are doing before you begin writing. Use the essay structure itself to design your paper; sort topics into the introduction, body sections, and conclusion. This is a careful problem-solving process, in which you refine the thesis, decide what comes first in the body, decide where facts and quotes will appear in the argument. Once you know the details of the three sections of the essay, you can begin writing.

3. Write a first draft, not a rough draft.

Do not write a *rough draft*; even a first draft should be excellent—not rough. Students often write bad first drafts if they do poor jobs of step two; they try to write without planning. That never works; you cannot skip the outlining or organizing stage.

Why not? If your first draft is not well-planned, if it is rough, then that means it is rough not only because it has bad sentences but because it is structurally disorganized.

You wind up working on *it*, fighting a bad structure, and the original bad structure you wrote, your rough structure, grows into the rough structure of the final paper. You can paint mud, but it is still mud. Once you write that rough structure down, it never goes away. So do not write a rough draft; instead, write a superb-quality first draft. With that as your foundation, you have something great to revise and proofread.

Your attitude of academic scholarship will be your guide at this stage; you must have a fierce determination to create an excellent foundation for your paper. Using your outline or essay plan as a guide, write carefully, as though you knew you would not be able to revise. Write slowly, one word and sentence at a time; do not let your thoughts flow out hastily in blobs of uninspected sentences—the brainstorming stage in step two was the time for the rapid flow of ideas. Write the essay in clear sections: introduction, body, and conclusion. Use a key thesis word or two consistently to tie the sections together. Write clear transitions between paragraphs. Write a patient, thoughtful, and complete conclusion. Doing your first draft on a computer makes revision easier later.

4. Take a break, then revise.

Never—ever—turn in your first draft unless you want to be horrified when you get your paper back. Take a break; get away from the first draft until your mind clears and you can see what you have actually written. Once you can be objective, reread and revise the paper carefully. Almost certainly, the first draft will be too wordy, and you will be removing unnecessary words, or sentences, or even paragraphs. This is the stage where you might do some rearranging of sections or paragraphs, or of sentences within paragraphs.

5. Proofread. Repeat as necessary.

As we have seen, proofreading takes time. If you hurry, you will miss errors on every page of your paper, with disastrous results. Focus. You have to check each word and punctuation mark, each MLA detail. Make sure that you have not used any contractions, any slang or clichés, any first person, or any form of self-reference. Advanced academic proofreading requires a tough, disciplined mind. Decide that you are going to be good at this, that you are going to make it impossible for your teacher to catch you in an elementary English error or an MLA format error. Give your teacher a chance to enjoy your good thesis.

Assignment One • A Paper about a Poet

The Concept of the Paper

In high school and college you will almost certainly have to write papers about poets and poetry. You may also need to include poems in papers about other subjects. Now is the time to learn how to do that. You need experience with documenting poetry quotations properly, but more than that, you need to learn as much as you can about the importance of poetry in intellectual history. To deepen the exploration, we will require you to read biographies or other nonfiction about the poet you select.

Purpose: Thinking and Writing about Poetry

This paper will develop your ability to interpret poetic ideas using a combination of factual information and critical interpretation.

Topic: An Idea in Poetry Written before 1950

This is a scholarly paper, so the poetry you discuss may not be from a modern poem or song. Your teacher may also want to tie the topic to the course content, so if you are studying England, it may have to be a British poet. Shakespeare is one serious possibility.

As an example: suppose you decide to work on the poetry of a British poet. You might discover, as you read the poems carefully, that there is a consistent theme of optimism, or despair, or loyalty, or emptiness, that pervades the poems, tying them together. You could explore that, and perhaps find facts about the poet's life, or comments in the poet's letters, that help to explain the theme.

Length: Four Pages

This paper must be no more than four pages long, with a fifth page for the Works Cited. Page four should contain a half-page or more of text. This only amounts to about ten paragraphs and four long quotations, so it is not as big an assignment as it might seem.

Due Date: Your teacher will assign the date, providing at least two weeks for both research and writing. Late papers will lose one letter grade per day.

Format: MLA

This will be an MLA essay with long and short quotations. A paper done in any other format may not be accepted and may be returned to you to be redone. The teacher may assign a letter-grade-per-day penalty for lateness in such a case. The paper should be typed on one side of the page only, in ragged-right, double-spaced Courier type font, ten- or twelve-point size. There must be a minimum of two long quotations and four short quotations in the paper. There is no separate title page. Do not hole-punch your paper or put it in a plastic or cardboard folder; keep it professional-looking.

Structure: Essay

This paper should be a three-part thesis essay, with introduction, body, and conclusion. The paragraphs should be organized and clearly connected. Use a key word from your thesis to connect the paper.

Sources: Five Sources of Fiction and Nonfiction

For this paper you must have a minimum of five sources in your Works Cited page, including both books of poetry and supporting nonfiction books such as critical comment and biography.

Honor: Your Plagiarism Pledge

Before you turn your paper in, you should write on the back of the paper, "I know that plagiarism is the unacknowledged use of someone else's words or ideas, and I pledge that this paper is not plagiarized" and sign it. A plagiarized paper will receive a zero.

Teacher: Your Teacher Is the Authority

For all of these guidelines, your teacher has the final say. If he or she wants to amend any detail, that is final.

Mollie Fide

Ms. Cheevius

English Honors

9 October 2007

The Dissident Poetry of Jane Austen

Readers of Jane Austen's novels have always enjoyed her dissident observations about society's fatuous customs. In *Pride and Prejudice*, for example, the fortissimo Mrs. Bennet is obsessed with marrying her daughters to wealthy men, and Mr. Bennet provides constant retorts, at one point saying to his daughter Elizabeth, who had rejected a proposal of marriage from the tedious Mr. Collins, that:

> An unhappy alternative is before you, Elizabeth. From this day you must be a stranger to one of your parents. Your mother will never see you again if you do not marry Mr. Collins, and I will never see you again if you do. (Austen 192)

In Mr. Bennet's words, before his nonplussed wife, we detect the dissident spirit of the author, concealing more than a common disdain for the social rules that would force marriage for financial reasons.

In addition to her famous novels, however, Jane Austen wrote accomplished poetry that echoed her social concerns. One such poem, "When stretch'd on One's Bed," expresses Austen's utter weariness with the tedium of social events. The poem has five sestets, with the Spanish-style rhyme scheme of aabccb, and the second stanza brings the tedium of society to sharp focus: "How little one feels / For the walzes and reels / Of our dance-loving friends at a Ball!" (7-12). The second sestet strengthens the dissident sense of indifference to society's shallow concerns:

> How little one minds
> If a company dines
> On the Best that the Season affords!
> How short is one's muse
> O'er the Sauces and Stews,
> Or the Guests, be they Beggars or Lords. (13-18)

Works Cited

Austen, Jane. *Pride and Prejudice*. New York: Halfcourt, 2003.

---. "When Stretch'd on One's Bed." *Great Poems by Great Novelists.* Ed. Marcus Heavilly. New York: Rabble, 2001.

Ception, Dee. Introduction. *Poetic Devices in Jane Austen's Novels.* By A N. T...

SECOND PAPER: COMPARISON OR CONTRAST

Mort Almann

Ms. Teemorninn

English Honors

14 February 2006

The Contradictions of Alexander

Although there are dozens of biographies of Alexander the Great, there is a surprising and unresolved dichotomy of interpretation concerning the essential nature of Alexander. Was Alexander, as some believe, a heroic military genius and one of history's greatest leaders who brought Greek culture and enlightened tolerance to much of the ancient world, or was he, by grim contrast, a ruthless narcissist who annihilated and enslaved every nation that stood in the path of his ambition? Are we to find Alexander admirable or detestable?

Even in a cynical age, the heroic view of Alexander has its adherents. "Alexander," says Robert Teich, professor of ancient culture at Wyndham University, "did do things that would horrify us, but those actions were typical of the time. What was not typical of the time was the magnanimous and tolerant approach he took to those he had defeated" (Teich 87). Other scholars agree. Diane Radish, Lead Scholar for the Ancient Cultures Project, says that Alexander was "more extraordinary for his humanity than for his military genius" (Radish 352).

These positive assessments of Alexander's nature are supported by a collection of legends, such as Alexander's confrontation with the philosopher Diogenes the Cynic. According to the legend, Alexander found Diogenes in Corinth, lying in the warm morning sun. Alexander approached Diogenes, saying, "I am Alexander the Great":

"I am Diogenes, the Dog," he replied. Startled by Diogenes's fearlessness, Alexander said, "I will grant you one wish." "Then," said Diogenes, "move out of my sun." There was silence, then Alexander said, "If I were not Alexander the Great, I would ___ (Goodwrench 59)

___ted by Alexander's

Works Cited

Balderdash, Lotta. *Alexander the Great, the Horror, the Horror.* New York: Halfcourt, 2002.

Goodwrench, M.R. *Alexander and the Reinstatement of Heroism.* Atlanta: Bignet, 2009.

Radish, Diane. *The Legends of Alexander: Reading Between the ___* New York: Randall, 2001.

Use Academic Words

Here are ten more academic vocabulary words from *The Word Within the Word*, Volume Two. The numbers are chapter numbers where the words are found in that book.

	Word	Definition	Part of Speech	Example
36.	**assonance**	vowel repetition	noun	We heard the **assonance** of the *o*'s.
36.	*sui generis*	unique	adjective	The novel's style was *sui generis*.
37.	**lionize**	treat as a celebrity	verb	The champion was **lionized**.
37.	**assiduous**	persevering	adjective	She wrote with **assiduous** effort.
38.	**desultory**	rambling	adjective	The **desultory** monologue droned on.
38.	**reiterate**	repeat	verb	She **reiterated** her objection.
39.	**patrician**	aristocratic	adjective	His **patrician** tone offended her.
39.	**narcissism**	self-infatuation	noun	Wilde's **narcissism** was legendary.
40.	**maladroit**	clumsy	adjective	The **maladroit** compliment failed.
40.	**expository**	explanatory	adjective	The **expository** essay was unclear.

These words shows the human power of vocabulary. Who among us would wish to be called *patrician*, which does not necessarily but can suggest arrogance? Who would want to be called a *narcissist*, a person so self-involved that he or she is completely self-obsessed? How would you feel if you gave a speech, and someone called it *desultory*? Ouch. These are power words that describe people.

Mixed in with these human power words we see good words for intellectual discourse. The adjective *sui generis*, in italics above because it is Latin, means unique, one of a kind. To *reiterate*, another useful intellectual word, is to repeat; you will notice that I reiterate important points in this book.

Discussion question: Pick two words from this list that you believe you are most likely to use in a research paper about Mother Teresa, and explain why you chose them.

Write grammatically correct sentences.

Academic writers do not write obliviously, unaware of the construction of their sentences. Instead, there is a grammatical self-awareness that is one of the best pleasures of writing. Grammar lets you know—as you write it—that the sentence is correct, and you enjoy seeing the right pieces snap into place. This example is from *4Practice, Volume Two*:

From F. Scott Fitzgerald's *The Great Gatsby*, 1925

	Happy,	**vacuous**	bursts	of	laughter	rose	toward	the	summer	sky.
Parts of Speech	adj.	adj.	n.	prep.	n.	v.	prep.	adj.	adj.	n.
Parts of Sentence			subj.			AVP				
Phrases				----prep. phr.----			-----------------prep. phr.----------------			
Clauses	---one independent clause---									
				a simple declarative sentence						

Grammar: The adjective *summer* may seem to be a noun, but it modifies *sky*.

Vocabulary: The power adjective *vacuous* means mindless, stupidly empty of ideas. W37

Poetics: The *a* assonance of *happy* and *vacuous* prepares us to notice *laughter*: *hAppy vAcuous lAughter*. Notice the concentration of *r*'s in the laughter of the sentence: *buRsts laughteR Rose towaRd summeR*. *Notice bURsts laughtER*. The entire sentence is a metaphor.

Writing: There is a special poetic quality to Fitzgerald's sentences; they sound wonderful and clear. It is partly an effect of simple grammar, partly the restrained use of big words, partly the control of vowels and consonants, and partly the choice of perfect words, such as the one-syllable noun *bursts* in this sentence.

Punctuation: We see a comma separating two adjectives that precede a noun.

Actual Research Paper Comments

Let us now look at ten more actual research paper comments. Remember that these are real comments written as responses to real student papers. The point is that students have made these very errors frequently, so they are especially dangerous. In this group of comments, we will feature comments about good writing style.

```
1. Avoid unnatural wording.
```
Use natural-sounding language. A sentence such as "This idea supports the theory of Praeger" sounds unnatural and artificial. We would never say, in normal communication, "He saw the dog of Bob"; we would say, "He saw Bob's dog." Similarly, even in a formal research paper, you should write, "This idea supports Praeger's theory," not "the theory of Praeger." You should not be colloquial, or descend into slang; your language should be natural.

```
2. Avoid clichés.
```
Please use original language rather than clichés. In a formal paper, you should avoid using all clichés, which are standard phrases that everyone knows, such as "the upper hand," "ups and downs," "way ahead of his time," "in this day and age," "pretty far along," "the world as we know it," or "told him to his face." You would not say, for example, that you can almost "reach out and touch" the characters in Homer's vivid poems, because that phrase is a tired cliché that we have heard before. Express your idea in your own original words: In Homer's vivid poems, the characters seem so real that you feel you could touch their faces. See? You would not say that Hemingway's characters "give it their best shot." You can use the same idea, but by putting it in original language, you make it much more effective. In general, if you have heard a phrase before, then do not use it. Avoid all prefab, ready-made phrases and sayings. Make your sentences new; make up your own phrases and metaphors.

```
3. Avoid colloquial words.
```
Choose academic, not conversational, words. Please do not use slang or inappropriately informal language in a formal paper. The words you choose should be good, common academic words; you should not use lofty, stilted, or pompous diction. Avoid saying that we can "relate to" a book; rather, we can understand it. You should not say that Shakespeare was a "heavy guy," or that he wrote "a lot" of plays. In fact, please completely avoid using the term "a lot" in formal papers. Instead of "a lot," use a more appropriately serious word, such as "many." Shakespeare wrote MANY plays. Even a sentence such as "Aristotle thought that the best life should contain some tremendously great item" is too colloquial; it sounds like casual conversation rather than like the disciplined, formal tone of a research paper.

4. Avoid contractions.

Avoid contractions in formal writing. There is nothing incorrect about the grammar of a contraction, but the contraction is not in keeping with the serious intellectual tone of a formal essay. Contractions suggest that one is in a hurry and does not wish to write out each word separately. Of course, if there are contractions in a quotation you use, then you leave the contraction alone; I am only referring to the use of contractions in sentences you write yourself.

5. Use *and*, not + or &

Use the word *and* rather than a PLUS (+) or AMPERSAND (&). Sometimes students think that *and*, +, and & are all acceptable or interchangeable. In handwriting or even sometimes in typing, they write about "Socrates & Plato" or about "Socrates + Plato." But a plus is only a mathematical symbol representing addition, and an ampersand has limited use and should not be substituted casually for the word *and*. Write with words, not symbols.

6. Avoid *etc.*

Please avoid *etc.*, *etcetera*. Instead of putting the abbreviation *etc.* at the end of a list, say something concrete and specific, such as "and other forms of incompetence." Write with good complete words, not shortcuts such as abbreviations or contractions. Words feel more graceful than abbreviations. Do not give the reader the impression that you do not have time to be complete or specific; in a formal paper, you DO have time. Furthermore, even if you type out *etcetera*, you would still be better off to say something explanatory instead; the reader may or may not know what you intend by *etcetera*. It is better to be sure that you are clear than to assume that you are clear.

7. Avoid passive voice

Please avoid passive voice verb constructions. Instead of saying "What has been shown by Homer," say "What Homer has shown." Instead of saying "Dickens was honored by the Society," say "The Society honored Dickens." Instead of "Some examples are given by Durant," say "Durant gives four examples." Use an active voice verb and a direct object, rather than a passive voice verb and a prepositional phrase. Active voice gives your writing energy, vigor, and impact, whereas passive voice is lacking in those qualities. Passive voice can be a particular problem in the sentences you use to introduce quotations, where there is a tendency to say something like, "It is written by William Simon that . . .." Active voice would be better: "William Simon notes that . . .."

8. Do not address the reader as "you."

Do not address the reader as "you." This is a formal paper that explores an idea; it is not a private communication that is addressed to a single individual; therefore, it has a different tone; the reader is not expecting suddenly to read a reference to himself or herself. Instead of writing, "You have to remember that dreaming alone never accomplished anything," write "Perhaps dreams alone never accomplished anything." Leave out the second person pronoun.

9. Write graceful segues.

Write graceful segues to introduce your quotations. Do you know the sentence you write just before a quotation in order to lead in to the quotation? Well, let us call that a *segue*, pronounced SEGG-way. A common problem that beginning writers have is the inability to write a graceful segue. There are three special varieties of the bad segue: one is the boring repetitive segue, in which the student uses the same phrase to introduce every quotation (He stated . . ., He stated . . ., He stated . . ., *ad infinitum*). A second special variety of the bad segue is the awkwardly worded segue, such as "This is what Dickens says when he quotes the statement that says . . ." A third variety of the bad segue is the passive voice segue: "It is stated by Richard Lattimore that . . ." Active voice would be better: "Richard Lattimore states that . . ." Please work on the economy, variety, and the grace of your segues. Use few words, make them sound natural and pleasant, and vary them. Examples include such phrases as, "Dickens explained: In Shakespeare's words: Perhaps Steinbeck described it best: Hemingway disagreed: James pointed out an interesting corollary: " and so on. You want the thoughts to flow naturally and pleasantly from your text into the quote.

10. Write out numbers.

Rather than using numerals to indicate small numbers in your paper, it is best to write the numbers from one to ninety-nine as words. The reason for this is that our work is literary rather than mathematical in nature, and so we use words rather than numbers. Instead of writing "When Sophocles was 28," write "When Sophocles was twenty-eight."

All of these comments have to do with academic style. Academic language has a certain dignity, avoids short-cuts, focuses on its topic rather than its author, expresses assessments of truth rather than high emotion or sentimentalism, and avoids communicating through worn-out common phrases. The more your read academic books and journals, the more you will feel the right sound of academic language and become able to write it.

Discussion Question:
Which of the comments is the biggest surprise to you? Why?

Advanced Thinking

If you have grown up reading encyclopedias, it is easy to think that the typical encyclopedia article is a good model for the academic papers you will write in high school and college. In fact, encyclopedia articles are bad models to have in mind. The academic essays we will write, and that teachers and professors will assign to you in the future, are nothing like most encyclopedia articles.

Why not? Our papers are different in purpose, in content, and in structure. For example, many students, when asked to write a paper about the ideas of a famous individual, will begin this way: "Charles Dickens was born on February 7, 1812."

Disaster. From the first sentence, it is clear that the paper is no essay.

An academic essay is *not a list of chronological facts*. Think about it. A list of facts, in the order of their dates, is a one-part structure. Our papers are essays: three-part structures, with introductions, bodies, and conclusions. Furthermore, each of our papers has a thesis, but the encyclopedia fact article is only a set of facts that does not make a case for an idea. It is only a report of facts. Our papers *use* facts, but they are not *about* facts; our papers are about *ideas*. That is why they are organized differently; they are organized not chronologically but in a sequence that best makes the idea-case.

When I first began assigning research papers to my students, they kept turning in fact reports. They had never read research papers, but they had read encyclopedia articles, and so they wrote papers modeled on the encyclopedias they had read. They did not understand what I wanted their papers to be about, so I finally wrote the handout you see on the following page, and gave a copy to each student. What the handout shows, in brief, is that in these papers you cannot simply report facts. Even though it must contain plenty of facts, your paper has to be *about* ideas. You can report ideas, you can report and evaluate ideas, or you can even report and create ideas. Any of those three plans, if done well, can result in an outstanding paper. Study the handout carefully.

ADVANCED THINKING IN RESEARCH

1. CREATION OF IDEAS

A. Production of an elaborate new and original critical or interpretive idea, theory, or model. A highly elaborated original idea regarding the subject researched, with possible brief presentation of preexisting ideas as a framework for presentation of the new idea. An elaborate, detailed case made for the validity of the original idea, based on factual, logical, and or expert evidence also discovered in research. Example: The undiscovered theme in the plays of Bernard Shaw.

B. Comparison of researched ideas with self-created interpretation of ideas. An elaborate comparison of competing researched ideas, supporting neither, resolving in favor of a more valid original critical or interpretive idea, theory, or model, with a case made for the validity of the original idea. Example: The inadequacy of three theoretical models of social mobility, with a new model suggested.

2. EVALUATION OF IDEAS

A. Evaluation of compared competing ideas. Close comparison of two or more competing ideas discovered in research, with a case made supporting some, one, or none of the ideas, on the basis of factual, logical, and or expert evidence also discovered in research. Example: Why the particle theory of gravity is a better model than the wave theory of gravity.

B. Evaluation of an idea discovered in research. Close examination of an idea discovered in research, with a case made for or against the idea, on the basis of factual, logical, and or expert evidence also discovered in research. Example: A refutation of J.M. Whistler's attacks on the originality of Oscar Wilde's theories of art.

3. REPORTING OF IDEAS

A. Comparison of competing ideas. Close comparison or contrast of two or more competing ideas discovered in research, analyzing and enumerating the differences between the ideas. Example: The contrast between Voltaire's Enlightenment-based philosophy and the optimism of Leibnitz, whom Voltaire ridiculed.

B. Thesis report of a researched idea. A presentation of a critical or scholarly idea, with no attempt to evaluate the validity of the idea, to compare it with other competing theories, or to challenge the idea with evidence or ideas of one's own. Example: Randall Jarrell's interpretation of the poetry of Robert Frost.

---

4. REPORTING OF FACTS ONLY (NOT ALLOWED)

Though there is a scholarly place for high-quality factual reports, I do not allow students to do them as research papers in my class. I think that students need to learn to discuss ideas, and that the research paper is a good opportunity for them to practice articulating literary and intellectual ideas.

A. Theme biographical fact report.
A report of factual information clearly and intelligently organized around a central theme. No production of original ideas. This variety is not acceptable in a research paper for my class, since I wish you to focus your discussion on ideas, rather than facts. Example: Charles Dickens's relationship with his family.

B. Encyclopedia-style themeless chronological biographical fact report.
Inappropriate for advanced scholarship. Example: The life of Charles Dickens, from birth to death.

Proofreading Practice: Good Style Is Clean

"After long thought and much perplexity, to be very brief was all that she could determine on with any confidence of safety." - Jane Austen, *Northanger Abbey*

"And so it went, the inexorable elimination of the superfluous." - Jack London, *The Call of the Wild*

"If you see an adjective, kill it." - Mark Twain

"The adverb is not your friend." - Steven King

"If it is possible to cut a word out, always cut it out." - George Orwell

It would be possible to overwhelm you with rules and guidelines about good writing style. In fact, we just studied ten actual research paper comments about style, and it would be easy to list many more. All of these guidelines are valid and important, but they are, in a sense, too close to the problem. The point-by-point approach is like trying to see a building, when your nose is only one inch from it. To understand what good style is, we need to step away until we can see the entire problem in our field of vision. Then we can see how all of those little rules point in the same direction.

The essence of good style is to say only what you mean.

When you write your first draft—even an outstanding first draft—you will not notice your pointless adjectives, phrases, and sentences. Later, when you are editing and proofreading, cut down to the meaning. Rarely will you improve a draft by adding words; the job is to remove words that do not earn their keep. Replace *giant statue* with *colossus*. Changed *screamed loudly* to *shrieked*. Change *the voice of the people* to *the people's voice*. Keep collapsing the sentences to their cores of meaning.

When you cut away all distracting, noisy, unnecessary words, that leaves the right words alone on the page. Then your reader cannot miss your point because there is nothing but your point left. What words would you remove from the essay on the next page?

Ella Gantlee

Ms. Nomer

English Honors

14 February 2008

Mondrian's Dogma of Square Reality

Friends of the incredibly modern abstract painter Piet Mondrian tell a fascinating story that when Mondrian went for a walk in the woods, he would walk in very straight lines and turn at right angles (Sampson 73). The story is believable in light of Mondrian's paintings, which with their dark, black lines crisscrossing at right angles, punctuated by rectangles of color, convey an almost dogmatic, rigid view of reality. Mondrian, who wore a correct suit and tie even while painting, was said to be "stiff and formal" (Jacobs 159) in social interactions, and the totally unavoidable implication is that Mondrian, a Calvinist, probably viewed not only spatial reality but moral reality in terms of right angles. Audrey Ellison, the curator of the Mondrian Museum in Amsterdam (Mondrian was born in Holland), says that Mondrian's:

> . . . view of both physical and spiritual reality was captured in the stark right angles of his later paintings. The images seem to say that this IS the truth, and other ideas are simply forms of denying the obvious. (Ellison 292)

Mondrian died in 1944 at the advanced age of seventy-two. One of the real implications of this date is that he lived much of his esteemed life before Albert Einstein published his amazing theory of relativity; Mondrian, therefore, was living in a world still dominated by Newtonian physics, which viewed reality in three dimensions of physical space. Mondrian, in other words, "lived in a Euclidean-Newtonian mental environment of height, width, and depth, measurable with rectilinear geometry" (Raphael 95), and this squared geometrical form of perception, which would soon be completely shattered by Einstein's outstanding discoveries and the development of tensor calculus, would dominate his artistic view of the actual world.

Assignment Two • Compare or Contrast Ideas

The Concept of the Paper

In literature, history, and science courses, you may be asked to write papers comparing one idea to another. You might be asked to compare and contrast idealism and pragmatism, or to show how Jane Austen's character Elizabeth Bennet is different from Charlotte Brontë's character Jane Eyre, or how Mary Shelley's Frankenstein monster is similar to Mark Twain's character Huckleberry Finn. You might be asked to explore points of conflict between the particle theory of matter and the wave theory in physics. These papers force you to think between the ideas and to discover thoughts of connection that are not visible if you look at one side alone.

Purpose: **Comparing or Contrasting Ideas**

This paper will take you deeper into your existing course of study and will develop your ability to compare or contrast academic ideas.

Topic: **A discipline-based comparison.**

Your teacher will decide which discipline this paper will explore. To give three examples:

Literature: If the area is literature, you might compare the literary themes of two different novelists, or the moral thinking of two different characters from their novels.

History: If the subject is history, you might compare the governing styles of two famous leaders, the strategies of two military geniuses, or the merits of two different policies.

Science: In science you might compare the survival traits of two biological forms, or the main ideas of two famous scientists.

Length: **Four Pages**

This paper must be four pages long with an additional page for the Works Cited. Page four should contain a half-page or more of text.

Due Date: Your teacher will assign the date, providing at least two weeks for both research and writing. Late papers will lose one letter grade per day.

Format: MLA

This will be an MLA essay with long and short quotations. A paper done in any other format will not be accepted but will be returned to you to be redone. The teacher may assign a letter-grade-per-day penalty for lateness in such a case. The paper should be typed on one side of the page only, in ragged-right, double-spaced Courier type font, ten- or twelve-point size. There must be a minimum of two long quotations and four short quotations in the paper. There is no separate title page.

Structure: Essay

This paper should be a three-part thesis essay, with introduction, body, and conclusion. The paragraphs should be organized and clearly connected. Use a key word from your thesis to connect the paper.

Sources: Five Sources of Fiction and Nonfiction

For this paper you must have a minimum of five sources in your Works Cited page.

Honor: Your Plagiarism Pledge

Before you turn your paper in, you should write on the back of the paper, "I know that plagiarism is the unacknowledged use of someone else's words or ideas, and I pledge that this paper is not plagiarized" and sign it. A plagiarized paper will receive a zero.

Teacher: Your Teacher Is the Authority

For all of these guidelines, your teacher has the final say. If he or she wants to amend any detail, that is final.

Ellah Vator

Ms. Tearyforce

English Honors

11 November 2006

Occam's Razor and the Bermuda Triangle Myth

Among the hallowed principles of sensible thought is Occam's Razor, the idea that simple or obvious explanations are more likely to be true than complicated or forced explanations are. The principle was first articulated by William of Ockham, a logician and Franciscan friar of the 14th century who was born in the English village of Ockham. Ockam's statement was that "Entities should not be multiplied unnecessarily" (Berglitz 66). Isaac Newton's famous statement of Occam's Razor was that: "We are to admit no more causes of natural things than such as are both true and sufficient to explain their appearances" (Newton 174).

Occam's Razor is effective in helping us evaluate the so-called mystery of the Bermuda Triangle, which claims that in a corner of the Atlantic Ocean, the forces of nature are frequently reversed, causing ships and airplanes to vanish without a trace. Occam's Razor reveals that in order to believe the story of the Bermuda Triangle, one must accept a complicated list of improbable assumptions, none of which seem to be true anywhere in the world, and none of which are as probable as ordinary, more probable, explanations. Raddison Yardcourt, Director of the Ocean Sciences Project at Northlipton University, says that:

> Nothing ever seems to vanish mysteriously and suddenly as we are watching. There are no greater statistics of shipwreck or plane crash in the Atlantic than elsewhere. There are ships everywhere in the Atlantic always, but none of them has ever observed a reversal of nature off on the horizon. The Atlantic routes are popular among airline pilots. (Yardcourt 74)

Yardcourt offers a telling tautology that "There is no reason to believe something if there is no reason to believe it" (89), particularly when obvious and believable reasons, such as storms, darkness, mechanical failure, pilot inexperience, and fuel shortage are known to have been

Use Academic Words

Here are ten more academic vocabulary words from *The Word Within the Word*, Volume Two. The numbers are chapter numbers where the words are found in that book.

	Word	Definition	Part of Speech	Example
41.	**expatiate**	to elaborate	verb	He **expatiated** at long length.
41.	**ineffable**	inexpressible	adjective	He felt an **ineffable** sadness.
42.	**malefic**	causing harm	adjective	Iago's influence was **malefic**.
42.	**punctilio**	point of conduct	noun	He observed every **punctilio**.
43.	**truculent**	fiercely savage	adjective	His **truculent** response shocked us.
43.	**obloquy**	verbal abuse	noun	Hardy endured the critics' **obloquy**.
44.	**opprobrium**	disgrace	noun	His reputation sank into **opprobrium**.
44.	**tautology**	needless repetition	noun	"Widow woman" is a **tautology**.
45.	**expostulate**	earnestly object	verb	She **expostulated** against the rule.
45.	**pungent**	sharp	adjective	It was a **pungent** smell of ammonia.

Look carefully at this third group of words as we reflect on what they illustrate. It is not that this is a group of words you must memorize, though that would be a good idea. The point is that these words are examples of a class of words, academic words, that can teach you what academic vocabulary sounds like. I do not mean that you should put three or four such words in every sentence—far from it—but notice what these words are *not*. Notice how different *truculent*, *malefic*, *ineffable*, and *tautology* are from words such as *awesome*, *totally*, *couldn't*, or *cool*. Notice how different in tone these words are from tiresome clichés like "no way, shape, or form." Furthermore, would you feel comfortable using these academic words in the same sentence with a contraction? *Did not* is academic; *didn't* is not. *Person* and *individual* are academic; *guy* and *dude* are not. Look at these two sentences:

> Mr. Hyde was a truculent brute who did not mind the pain he inflicted.
> Mr. Hyde was a brutal guy who didn't care at all if he hurt people.

Discussion question: You write the way you read. If you rarely read academic writing, you will have no example in your mind. What is a good way to acquire reading experience with academic writing that includes words like those at the top of this page?

Write Grammatically Correct Sentences

It is always fun to see a sentence like this one, where the verb precedes its subject, and the beat is kept by the adverb *there*. This sentence is from *4Practice, Volume Two*:

From Mark Twain's *The Prince and the Pauper*, 1882

	There	were	middle-sized	youths	of	**truculent**	countenance.
Parts of Speech	adv.	v.	adj.	n.	prep.	adj.	n.
Parts of Sentence		LVP		subj.			
Phrases					--------------------prep. phr.-----------------		
Clauses	--one independent clause--- a simple declarative sentence						

Grammar: The first reaction is to see *were*, know it is a linking verb, and then think *youths* is a subject complement; but we look again and realize that the clause begins with the adverb *there*, used when the verb precedes the subject.

Vocabulary: The adjective *truculent* means fiercely savage, eager to fight; *truc* means fierce, and *lent* means full of. W43

Poetics: Notice the effective falling meter: THERE were / MIDD le sized / YOUTHS of / TRUC ulent / COUNT en ance. In poetry we would read this as trochee, dactyl, trochee, dactyl, dactyl. All feet end unstressed. Notice how well the vowels and consonants of *truculent* and *countenance* align: TruCuleNT CouNTenance.

Writing: We see a familiar technique: putting the power words at the end.

Punctuation: Without the hyphen in *middle-sized*, we might imagine that there were sized youths.

Actual Research Paper Comments

Let us now look at ten more actual research paper comments. This time let us focus on how ideas are displayed in an academic paper. This includes not only the quality of the ideas themselves, but also how format and structure contribute to the successful presentation of your ideas.

1. Analyze your quotations.
One technique I would like you to develop is the analysis of quotation. In other words you need to follow a long quotation--and sometimes a short one--with a comment, because you cannot assume that the meaning of the quotation has been obvious to the reader. The reader might not have understood the significance of the quotation, so you cannot just quote and go. Though it need not be a rigid (boring) pattern that you follow mechanically, you should frequently use a three-part structure in presenting quotations. First, introduce the quote with a sentence or paragraph that the quotation will illuminate, develop, or verify. Second, present the quotation, properly edited if necessary with [brackets] to show insertions and . . . ellipsis to show deletions (we edit quotes to remove irrelevant material and to make the language flow well from text to quote). Third, follow the quotation with a comment, explanation, or analytical breakdown of the quotation. The comment will often use short requotes, snipped from the quotation, to highlight important ideas. These short requotes should be placed in quotation marks, but they may be used freely without parenthetical documentation, since the documentary note has already been given in the full quote above. By providing this clarifying analysis after the quotation, you can make sure that the reader understands its meaning, and you can provide a logical bridge from this idea to the idea you plan to feature in your next paragraph.

2. Give evidence or avoid unfounded claims.
There are certain assertions you should not make unless you can provide evidence for them, especially in a formal paper where you are not allowed to present something as a fact if it is not one. It is risky to make assertions about what most people think, or about what a famous person thought or intended. How do you know what most people think? How do you know what was in the mind of another person? Unless you have some way to document such questionable assertions, avoid them.

3. Identify your sources.
It is a good idea to identify names the reader might not recognize, especially when you are first referring to authors and experts at the beginning of a research paper. If the person is important to your argument, you might write a sentence or even a paragraph explaining who the person is, as well as a brief explanation of how the expert's views are important to your thesis. If the source does not

play a major part in your paper, then use a briefer identification, such as a graceful appositive after the name or a quick prepositional phrase before it. You might say, "Ian Hamilton, author of the biography *Robert Lowell*, disagrees." Or: "In his biography *Robert Lowell*, Ian Hamilton notes that . . . ." It is unsettling for a reader to be faced with many unidentifiable names, so if your source is really an authority, then you want your reader to know why.

4. Include your analysis

There is a missing element in the ideas that this paper contains. Consider: What you have done is (1) to present examples as evidence and (2) to present expert opinion. You have, in essence, constructed a structure that displays other people's thoughts. What is still missing is your own scholarly analysis of the evidence you present. Learn to discuss your examples after you present them, and to discuss the opinions of experts as well. Take the time to zoom in, to do close-ups on the evidence. In other words, the object of research is not to collect examples and expert opinions; it is to use examples and expert opinions as a means of making your own assertion persuasive, of backing up your thesis. Include all three.

5. Avoid logical contradiction.

I have placed an (X) symbol to show that you have logically contradicted yourself. Probably you did not think contradictory thoughts, but you have worded your sentences so that you express contradictory thoughts. In a formal paper it is the expression of thoughts that is most important. You cannot expect a reader to guess what you think. Look closely at the passage I have marked, and you will find that what you have actually written means the opposite of what you meant to write.

6. Do not misquote. (quote?)

I have written *Quote?* on your paper to indicate a quotation that seems to be flawed. As you have it written, the quotation does not make sense, and I think that you have made an error in transcribing it. Either you mispunctuated, omitted a word or words, added a word or words, or changed words; any of these could have happened. It is also possible that you simply do not understand what the quotation means, and you have unwittingly tried to place it in a context in which it no longer makes sense. Without seeing the page you copied from, I cannot be sure what happened. In the future, please be sure to quote with perfect precision.

7. Use past tense for past subjects.

Use past tense verbs to describe the past. Though many students are tempted to use present tense in writing research papers, especially if the papers are about the works or literary ideas of writers, it is often advisable to use past tense instead. Past tense seems to be more manageable and to result in fewer tense parallelism errors, and past tense is the logical tense to use in describing an author who has been dead for centuries, such as Shakespeare. A verb's tense is part of what it predicates about its subject--part of the claim made by the sentence, and so there is something slightly jarring about a sentence such as, "Shakespeare writes his sonnets in a different sonnet form than Spencer," because we are aware that Shakespeare is not a living writer, as the tense of the sentence seems to imply. To say that "Aristotle believes in following the Golden Mean" is disturbing to our awareness that Aristotle is dead. Strictly speaking, it is false that Aristotle believes in the Golden Mean, but it is true that he believed in it. Although we sometimes employ a literary convention that allows us to speak of dead authors in the present tense, it is perhaps best to match each verb's tense to the truth, and to speak of past things in past tense.

8. Paraphrase properly.

Be careful with paraphrasing. Paraphrasing is giving a short summary or significant rewording of someone else's work. You might paraphrase because to quote would take too much space, as, for example, if you are condensing several pages or more down into one paragraph. Or you might paraphrase because the printed passage does not work if treated as a quotation; perhaps it is too scholarly or abstruse and needs clarification. But notice that paraphrase is NOT a near-quotation. You should never almost quote by only slightly changing a word here and there--this gives the false impression that you are the author of these sentences, when actually the real writer wrote them, and you have only barely modified them--a dishonest misrepresentation. If you are going to near-quote, then QUOTE.

It is also often difficult to tell where a student begins to paraphrase, so when you paraphrase an idea instead of quoting it, please use the following method: 1) Begin by naming--and if you have not already done so, identifying--the person whose idea it is. Example: In his *Story of Civilization*, Will Durant notes that . . . After you have named and identified the source, 2) Paraphrase the idea until you have accomplished what you wished. When you have finished paraphrasing, 3) Include a standard parenthetical documentary note containing name and page number (Durant 685). Put the period after the parenthetical note, not before it. Please understand that some instructors would not require you to name the source of your idea at the beginning, but I think it prevents confusion about which ideas are yours and which ideas are someone else's, and it completely protects you from charges of plagiarism.

9. Avoid simplistic reasoning

I say that your reasoning is simplistic not because you are wrong in your essential point but because you need to be careful about oversimplifying, about reducing what is obviously complicated and multifaceted into a too-easily explained answer. You want to avoid giving the reader the impression that you have not really looked deeply into the issue or have not considered all aspects of the problem. If the reader feels that there is obviously more to the problem than you seem to realize, then you are in trouble.

10. The sentence has its own meaning.
Remember that once you write a sentence, it means what it means--not what you mean. If you want to add 43 and 7 on a calculator, and you punch in 43 x 7, the calculator will give an answer of 301, not the 50 you expected. A sentence is just like that. Its meaning has nothing to do with your private intentions; its meaning is based on ITS structure. The meaning of a sentence is based on the instructions contained in the grammatical structure, and if you enter the wrong instructions, the sentence will mean something different from what you are thinking. A common example is a misplaced modifier that makes your meaning ridiculous: "Raising the American flag over Iwo Jima, the Japanese defenders watched the small group of American soldiers." This sentence means that it was Japanese soldiers who raised the American flag--an obviously ridiculous statement.

    The poor reader cannot be expected to guess what you mean; the reader has only the sentence to read, and the meaning that comes to the reader's mind will be based on the sentence--as though you did not exist. So when you write a sentence, you must perform a feat of advanced concentration in which you completely silence that part of you that knows what you mean; then you must look blankly at the sentence from the reader's perspective and change the words and structure until its meaning is accurate exactly as it is stated. It is the sentence that counts; the reader reads the sentence, not your mind.

As you see from these actual research paper comments, everything you do in an academic paper contributes to the success of your ideas. You can derail your idea with bad grammar or with a poor choice of words. You can be so wordy that the reader is unable to find your point in the confusion. You can fail to organize your paper in a logical (understandable) sequence. You can be so blinded by your own thinking that you scribble down sloppy sentences, not noticing as you have written them that they do not say what you think they do. You can fail to give enough facts or evidence for your thesis. You can choose quotations that are irrelevant, or that you have not read carefully enough. You can present faulty logic. You can even select a thesis that everyone already knows, and that needs no proof. Everything—everything—must be done with care.

Discussion Questions:

Which of the comments would you be most likely to receive on a paper you had written? Which of the comments is the most important? Why?

Good Writing: Use Words That Inform

One fault of bad writing is empty words. The result of poor word choice is that the paper can be unclear, uninteresting, or even irritating. It is worth our time now to think about word choice in some detail. Words should be academic and formal, but here are some additional principles for good word choice that you should be able to apply at once:

Use specific words. The more vague, general, or abstract you are, the less your sentences mean. If you say that someone began life as a worker, what does that mean? If you say that he was a blacksmith, or a stonemason, or a carpenter, then we will understand. What if you say that someone had an illness? This will only irritate your reader, who is wondering, "What illness?" Say that the person had pneumonia, or tuberculosis. If the book you are reading only says *illness*, then find another book. Why say that someone was a relative of the author? Was she a cousin? An aunt? Then say that. Rather than say someone was born in the 18th century, can you find out the year? 1756 is better. Was someone an official in the government? Find out what office the person held, then you can say that she was the Assistant Attorney General. That is more interesting because it is more informative. In most cases you are only replacing one general word for one specific word, so your paper is not longer; it is more substantive.

Use precise words. Yes, San Juan is a heavily populated city, but you would be better to say that it has a population of nearly 450,000. Yes, the house is green, but it would be more interesting if we knew the color more precisely; is it emerald green? Is it a yellow-green, or a pea green? Yes, light is fast; that is true, but it is better to say that light goes a million miles in five seconds. Yes, the sound is loud, but is it a roar, a screech, a bang; is it thunderous?

Words are knowledge. Notice what happens when you choose words that are specific and precise: the effort to do that causes you to substitute empty general words with facts. Your paper becomes more interesting because it is more informative. General words give the impression that you do not know what you are talking about. Be as detailed as you can be. With specific and precise words, you are really telling your reader the details, rather than giving the impression that you did not bother to look the facts up.

Proofreading Practice

We have seen that proofreading is not what the beginner may assume. It is not a brief concluding task; rather, it is a patient, intense, multi-layered examination that makes your paper good enough to be published (or turned in).

We have looked at proofreading from the point of view of grammar, of punctuation, and of MLA format. Let us add to those the questions of wordiness and word choice. Here is a list of elements to check as you proofread the MLA page opposite and its Works Cited page below. How many errors can you find? Notice that every error makes you stop reading.

- ❏ Grammar
- ❏ Usage
- ❏ Punctuation
- ❏ MLA format
- ❏ Essay structure
- ❏ Connectedness, flow
- ❏ Academic tone
- ❏ Wordiness
- ❏ Word choice

Works Cited   Torius, 5

Ato, Tom, and C.M. Laff . *An Absurd Selection of Twentieth Century Prose.*
New York: Halfcourt University Press, 2001.

Runn, C. Howie. Introduction. *The Curiouser and Curioser Life of Franz
Kafka.* By G.D. Twoshoes. Chicago. Lakeview, 2002.

Kafka, Franz. *The Metamorphosis and Other Tales of the Absurd.* New York:
Redoubt, 2002.

Mantlee, Adam. "Gregor Samsa: The Sanity of Psychosis." *The Modern
Fiction Journal.* 2 (2005): 18-36.

Sprat, Jack. *Samsa Is a Bug.* Edinburg: Moray. 2006.

Torius, 1

Mary Torius

Ms. Feezance

English Honors

6 March 2009

KAFKA'S METAMORPHOSIS METAPHOR

Franz Kafkas' novel The Metamorphosis, first published in 1915, is one of the staples of world Literature, it the story of a salesman, Gregor Samsa, who wakes up in his bed to find that he has been metamorphosed into a really enormous insect, lying on it's back, with six legs wiggling in the air of his bedroom:

> He lay on his armour-like back, and if he lifted his head a little he could see his brown belly, slightly domed and divided by arches into stiff sections. The bedding was hardly able to cover it and seemed ready to slide off any moment. His many legs, pitifully thin compared with the size of the rest of him, waved about helplessly as he looked (Kafka 4).

The details of the story are clear enough; what is not clear is the interpretation, the meaning of the story. What has happened to this guy? Is The Metamorphosis a story of a man who is physically changed into an insect or is it the story of a man who is driven by emotional pain and loneliness into insanity. In which he sees himself metaphorically as he believes others see him? Is The Metaporphosis a metaphor? Each view--the physical view and the metaphorical view--have adherents, but there is more reason to accept the metaphorical interpretation.

Adam Mantlee, a professor of modern literature at Friesburg University takes the metaphorical view; he sees Kafka's story as "the metaphorical epitome of modern Alienation. It is a fictional expatiation of the malefic effects of individual loneliness in the presence of an absurd and pitiless society" (Mantee, 52). Ignoring individuals, Mantlee argues that sociaty is insane in it's indifference to the lives of other's, and that Gregor Samsas delusions are an escape from social insanity.

In contrast to Mantlee's metaphorical view, Jack Sprat, the author of Samsa is a Bug, compares The Metamorphosis to Mary Shelley's tragic tale

Evaluating Ideas

It is one thing to write an academic paper that presents an idea without attempting to solve whether or not the idea is valid. It is more challenging to go beyond reporting an idea to evaluating its merit. Perhaps you are writing a paper about Franz Kafka's novel *The Metamorphosis*, and you read a literary critic who argues that the novel is a metaphor for the loneliness and isolation of modern life. You can choose to report that idea, or you can choose to evaluate it, to make a case, let us say, for the idea. To do that, you might find other important critics who agree, and you might present a number of passages from the novel itself that give weight to the interpretation. As in most academic papers, you wind up piecing together statements that you find in a number of books and arranging them in your own way to back your case.

You will do all of this, remember, without ever mentioning yourself. You will not say, "In *my* opinion this idea is valid," or "*This paper* will show..." or "*I* agree with Smith's interpretation of Kafka." Rather than making any reference to yourself or your paper, you will simply direct the reader's mind at all times to Kafka and the other writers. You will say, "Smith's interpretation of Kafka reveals hidden details of meaning."

A milestone in intellectual life is when you discover that you cannot believe something simply because you read it in a book. The more you read, the more you realize that books (writers, in other words) do not agree, and so it becomes necessary to wait, to read with a skeptical mind, postponing judgment until you know the quality of the facts and reasons involved. You also learn to read more than one book. The next author might (and usually does) include something that the first author left out.

Evaluation is an important ability to develop because the world is filled with attempts to deceive us. There are attempts to persuade us for political reasons, including distracting us from major national issues with sensational (straw man) topics that go unmentioned between elections. There are weird science fiction stories that attempt to make large profits by pretending to be real science. There are hosts of products that lure us into purchases with deceptively worded advertisements ("No sugar added" is my favorite; this does not mean that the product has no sugar). There are phony experts who pretend to have authoritative knowledge that is really only partisan bias.

To make the problem more complex, there is no one set of criteria that can always be used to evaluate ideas or to compare them to one another. Literary ideas are evaluated differently from scientific ideas, and the evaluation of historical ideas is different still. You cannot evaluate the quality of a poem, or compare the quality of one poem to another, in the same way that you would evaluate an idea of philosophy or a theory of gravitation. Therefore, in addition to any criteria that I give you for evaluating or comparing ideas, your teacher may want to add special, course-specific dimensions that you can use to assess what you learn. Even with all of these qualifications, there are a few sensible things to consider when you are attempting to evaluate ideas:

Quality of sources. Not all books and magazines are of equal quality. When you write a serious academic paper, you go in search of serious academic sources—real scholarship, not just something invented to increase sales. This means, often, that you turn to articles and books by university researchers or by nationally recognized experts. Strong sources often have few illustrations, longer page length, academic sentences, academic vocabulary, and other academic apparatus such as indexes, footnotes, or bibliographies (Works Cited). These sources are not on the shelves in supermarkets or drug stores; you will find them in libraries or in excellent bookstores.

Common Sense. Evaluating ideas involves common sense, what we used to call using your head. A simple example is the profitable genre of sensational science mystery programs, deceptively presented as nonfiction, that pretend to examine the "evidence" for populations of large but for some reason uncatchable monsters, either on land or sea. Notice what happens when there really are large animals in the wild: no one has difficulty finding Komodo Dragons, or mountain gorillas, or even giant squid, though it is from the frequently washed-up bodies of giant squid that we primarily know them. Yet program after program tries to persuade us that there is a population of enormous marine dinosaurs in Loch Ness, as large as whales, and that unlike all other animals known to us, these massive beasts avoid all scientifically valid forms of detection.

Consider the crop circles supposedly made by alien visitors from space, and forget for a moment that the pranksters who make them keep confessing; is it common sense to think that an alien being would go to the massive effort to cross intergalactic space, just to come here and mess with our grass? If we sent astronauts to another inhabited planet, and finally descended through the atmosphere of their planet, would we wait until they were not looking, spin their grass into circles, and zip off into space again? It would be the most expensive practical joke in the history of the universe.

Monster legends and alien myths are easy to see through. Your problem will be using common sense to detect well-written academic nonsense. As an example, 12,900 years ago there was a mass extinction in the northern hemisphere, including North America. Suddenly, all of the mammoths, saber-toothed tigers, and giant sloths died. One theory holds that a comet hit the Earth, killing the animals in a storm of dust and fire. Another theory holds that the Clovis people, who made beautiful stone spears and arrows, were such successful hunters that they killed all large animals in the hemisphere—at once. Now, let us use common sense: today there are far more human beings in the hemisphere than there were at that time, and today we have hunting weapons vastly more powerful than stone spears, but we have not killed all bears, or deer, or moose in the northern hemisphere. The Clovis theory does not makes sense. The latest findings show that the soil of 12,900 years ago contains high levels of iridium and nanodiamonds—which are found frequently in comets but not frequently on earth.

Expert Opinion. You may remember, earlier in this text, the quotation by the astronomer Carl Sagan, that "No one's say-so is evidence." Remember also the *ad hominem* error of logic: the identity of the person speaking is not by itself evidence for truth. Consider also that there are disagreeing experts on different sides of questions, so simply quoting one expert does not end a discussion. On the other hand, one of the primary strategies in a research paper is precisely to present quotations from scholars and other experts to support or explain our thesis. When you are evaluating the merit of an idea, look carefully at the credentials of the writers you read, and look to see if their views are supported by others in the field. If you can quote more than one expert, that will be a comfort. Quotations from several experts, supported by a strong factual argument, can make a persuasive case. If there is strong disagreement among experts, or the facts are unclear or of low confidence, then your evaluation would likely be that the idea does not have enough support to be convincing.

Factual support. In an academic paper, we form our conclusions after we have learned the facts, and we respect the facts. This is one of the reasons we read so much before writing; we search and then re-search to learn more facts. We do not sort through the facts and present only those that reinforce our bias; we are honest about the facts. We have intellectual integrity. What is a fact? One view, articulated by science historian James Burke in *The Day the Universe Changed*, is that the fact was born when the printing press was invented; the printing press allowed a detail to be widely reported, and then to be checked and confirmed by others. When something is checked by many observers, and the result is repeated and consistently confirmed, then we say that it is a fact. Facts are true details that are consistently observed, regardless of the identity of the observer. As you read through different books about your topic, you will soon notice some facts that all of the books confirm. These facts help you avoid boring generalities; they provide many of the concrete, specific words that make your writing more interesting.

One of the reasons for seeking serious academic sources is that some authors distort the facts; they omit facts that refute their claims, they report only facts that help their book sell, and they sometimes make up false facts. This is dishonest, but in a free society, it is legal. The pseudoscience author Erik Von Daniken, for example, wrote that ancient artifacts he had found showed alien astronauts visiting Earth; it turned out that he had paid a local craftsman to *make* the so-called artifacts, and then lied about what they were. His book made money, but it deceived its readers who trusted Von Daniken. His career descended into controversy and disgrace. Your teacher and librarian can help you find respectable books and journals. Learn to prefer quality scholarship.

More thinking. What you will notice from this discussion is that an evaluation paper is more challenging than a straight report. It is, in essence, easier to say something than it is to think it through and decide if it is true. It takes more thinking, more of our personal thinking, than a straight repetition of ideas. An evaluation paper puts us as academic scholars in a position similar to that of a detective, having to piece together the crime scene evidence, connect the dots, and decide what it all means. If you approach the challenge from an advanced point of view, rather than wanting to hurry and get the paper over with, then you can enjoy finding the facts, enjoy reading the different ideas, and enjoy using your mind in this impressive way. It is fun to be good at this, and with practice, you can be *very* good.

What evaluation is *not*. It is not moralistic, self-righteous, or judgmental. Evaluation is not preaching; never allow yourself to sermonize: "Plato was an important thinker, and we should all appreciate his great ideas" (This is baloney, and the student is just trying to fill the page). The evaluation is not about moral right and wrong; it is about scholarly merit. An evaluation paper is not an opportunity to pontificate or lecture other people about what they should do. Just as you do not refer to yourself, do not address the audience as *you* or give them instructions. Write an academic evaluation of an academic idea.

Assignment Three • Evaluating Ideas

The Concept of the Paper

Reporting, comparing, and contrasting ideas are valuable academic techniques, but we go to a higher level when we attempt to weigh the ideas and decide whether or not they are true. An evaluation paper uses criteria that are appropriate to the topic to assess the merit of an idea. This also includes reporting because you cannot weigh something you have not first explained, but it goes beyond reporting to an argument about the truth of the idea.

Purpose: Evaluating an Idea

This paper will once again take you deep below the surface of your course of study, leading you into significant background reading, and causing you to think about the validity of a course-related idea. In the process you will gain an increased command of the factual knowledge and an acquaintance with important academic thought about the topic.

Topic: A discipline-based evaluation

Your teacher will decide which discipline this paper will explore. You might be evaluating a literary topic, such as a theme that is attributed to a novelist, or a historical theory about the effect of individuals on society, or a scientific idea. Your teacher may provide you with the idea that you will assess, or you may be given the freedom to choose your own idea from what you find in research; this is the teacher's decision.

Length: Four Pages

This paper must be four pages long, with a fifth page for the Works Cited. Page four should contain a half-page or more of text.

Due Date: Provided by Teacher

Your teacher will assign the date, providing at least two weeks for both research and writing. Late papers will lose one letter grade per day.

Format: **MLA**

This will be an MLA essay with long and short quotations. A paper done in any other format will not be accepted but will be returned to you to be redone. The teacher may assign a letter-grade-per-day penalty for lateness in such a case. The paper should be typed on one side of the page only, in ragged-right, double-spaced Courier type font, ten- or twelve-point size. There must be a minimum of two long quotations and four short quotations in the paper. There is no separate title page.

Structure: **Essay**

This paper should be a three-part thesis essay, with introduction, body, and conclusion. The paragraphs should be organized and clearly connected. Use a key word from your thesis to connect the paper.

Sources: **Five Sources of Fiction and Nonfiction**

For this paper you must have a minimum of five sources in your Works Cited page.

Honor: **Your Plagiarism Pledge**

Before you turn your paper in, you should write on the back of the paper, "I know that plagiarism is the unacknowledged use of someone else's words or ideas, and I pledge that this paper is not plagiarized" and sign it. A plagiarized paper will receive a zero.

Teacher: **Your Teacher Is the Authority**

For all of these guidelines, your teacher has the final say. If he or she wants to amend any detail, that is final.

FOURTH PAPER: CREATING AN ACADEMIC IDEA

Arriah 1

Mal Arriah

Ms. Tagogg

English Honors

4 April 2008

Whitman's Song Changed Poetry

It is not often that one individual has such an impact on a creative field that the field is never the same again, that everyone involved in the field, and indeed the world at large, views the field with different eyes. There have been a number of great poets in American history, but only one has changed the very nature of poetry, not just in the United States but in the world, making it impossible to go back, and that is Walt Whitman.

According to Henry David, Thorow Professor of Literature at Blake University, when Walt Whitman wrote *Leaves of Grass*, he:

> . . . was no mere pioneer of modern poetry, he invented modern poetry, like Euclid founded mathematics or Herodotus invented history. Whitehead once said that the entire history of western thought is based on Plato, and I would add that Whitman is the Plato of modern poetry. Before Whitman the traditions of poetry had ossified, but he delineated a new poetic world. (David 74)

This view of Whitman as the father of modern verse is the standard view. Eleanor Radcliffe agrees: "Walt Whitman laid the foundation for the poetry we write today. He broke the mold. Whitman was not only before his time, he was from a different artistic cosmos than the poets of his time and before" (Radcliffe 73). F.G. Leghorn says that "Whitman changed everything. If you want to see the shift in poetry, look at any anthology before-poetry and the after-poetry" (Leghorn 134).

. . . that Whitman transformed the art of . . . do to poetry,

In the past the MLA method underlined titles; today, we use true italics instead.

Works Cited   Arriah 4

David, Henry. *Whitman Sang My Song*. New York: Halfcourt, 1992.

Leghorn, F.G. "How Walt Whitman Changed the Landscape of Poetry." Introduction. *Modern Poetry and the Song of Ourselves*. Chicago: Addem UP, 2003.

Radcliffe, Eleanor. *The Conceptual Foundations of Modern Poetry*. Atlanta: Bignet, 2008.

---. *Primary Themes in Poetry since 1800*. St. Paul: Simone, 1998.

Whitman, Walt. *The Complete Poetry of . . .*

Use Academic Words

Here are ten more academic vocabulary words from *The Word Within the Word*, Volume Two. The numbers are chapter numbers where the words are found in that book.

Word	Definition	Part of Speech	Example
46. **paragon**	excellent model	noun	She was a **paragon** of courtesy.
46. **antipathy**	strong dislike	noun	Voltaire felt **antipathy** for Leibnitz.
47. **pharisaism**	hypocrisy	noun	The **pharisaism** repelled the crowd.
47. **feckless**	without effect	adjective	Their efforts were tragically **feckless**.
48. **replete**	filled	adjective	The text is **replete** with examples.
48. **querulous**	complaining	adjective	The **querulous** objections continued.
49. **nonentity**	a nobody	noun	The character is a shallow **nonentity**.
49. **misnomer**	wrong name	noun	To call whales *fishes* is a **misnomer**.
50. **repartee**	witty reply	noun	*Cyrano* is filled with quick **repartee**.
50. **dissident**	one who disagrees	noun	Solzhnitsyn was a Soviet **dissident**.

Here are ten more strong words. Compare them with their definitions, and you will notice the decidedly more educated sound of the words. We see the noun *dissident*, which is frequently used in historical or political language. *Dissident* can also be an adjective, as when we call someone a *dissident writer*. *Querulous* is a good classic word; you will see it often in literature. The adjective *replete* has a strong Latin tone; it is rarely used in conversation, but is often used in academic writing. Some words, such as *antipathy* or *paragon*, might be found in almost any context, from a novel to a biography. The key is still to build your appreciation for such words, to take them in as friends. The more you identify yourself as someone who loves words, the more you position yourself for a strong intellectual life. An academic vocabulary makes it possible for you to participate in many academic contexts; without it, you will have difficulty understanding what is being said, or what you are reading, or how you should write. Be energetic and self-motivated about learning words.

Discussion questions: What two words in this list are least familiar to you? Which two do you feel most likely to encounter in your reading? Which two will be most fun to use? In each case, explain why you chose the ones you did.

Write Grammatically Correct Sentences

Continue to develop your sense of how a correct sentence is made. Think about the standard patterns and structures that are almost always present in a correct sentence. This sentence is from *4Practice, Volume Two*:

From Emily Brontë's *Wuthering Heights*, 1847

Parts of Speech										
My	young	lady	was	no	philosopher	and	no	**paragon**	of	patience.
adj.	adj.	n.	v.	adj.	n.	conj.	adj.	n.	prep.	n.

Parts of Sentence

subj.   LVP   S.C.   S.C.

Phrases

-----prep. phr.----

Clauses

--one independent clause--

a simple declarative sentence

Grammar: This is a wonderful example of how a linking verb equation can vary; we see a compound subject complement in which the equation is negated because each complement is modified by the power adjective *no*.

Vocabulary: A *paragon* is an excellent model, a perfect example; *para* means beside. W46

Poetics: We see excellent alliteration in *Paragon of Patience*.

Writing: As we often see in great writing, the sentence is perfect in that every word tells. There are no superfluous adjectives, but there is a precise choice of nouns in *philosopher* and *paragon*, that renders further adjectives unnecessary.

Punctuation: Here the lesson is the absence of punctuation; notice that a compound subject complement does not require a comma before the coordinating conjunction *and*.

Actual Research Paper Comments

Let us now look at ten more actual research paper comments. This time, let us look at an array of different important ideas.

1. Avoid choppy organization.

Your paper is difficult to read, not because it is disorganized but because the organization is choppy. You have chopped your main ideas into so many small paragraphs that the reader cannot distinguish large sections from small sections, cannot tell when a discussion of an idea is over, and cannot tell whether there are a few ideas being discussed in many paragraphs or there are many ideas being discussed. Try to have some correspondence between the idea structure and the paragraph structure and to avoid discussing a single idea in so many small paragraphs that the visual integrity of the idea on the page disintegrates.

2. Avoid pronoun reference errors.   (ref)

Make your pronouns agree with their antecedents. My *ref* mark means that you have a pronoun reference error which is a disagreement in number between a pronoun and its antecedent. Remember that you may never use the plural words *they*, *them*, *themselves*, or *their* to refer to an individual or to something that is singular. If you mean something, someone, no one, nobody, somebody, anyone, everyone, everybody, each person, every person, an individual, or any other singular reference, you may not use the plural pronoun. A person is not they; a person is he or she. Someone did not drop their book; someone dropped his or her book, or someone dropped a book. *Their* refers to them, and if they are not who you mean, do not imply that it is theirs! Please note that even plural-sounding words such as *everyone* and *everybody* are really singular, since they emphasize every-ONE. This is tricky when you first learn it.

3. Double-space your entire paper.

Please double-space your entire paper. The MLA rules call for you to double-space your entire paper, including the title-page information at the top left of the first page, the long quotes, and the Works Cited page. You should also only double-space down from the title to the first sentence of the paper, double-space down to and from each long quotation, and double-space from the header at the top of each page down to the first line of the page. Be careful not to use space-and-a-half or triple-spacing.

Note that in some methods long quotes may be single-spaced, but in the MLA method everything is double-spaced.

4. Header (Smith 3) instructions.

Make your page headers correctly. Please study the MLA page-numbering method.
You should type your last name, followed by one blank space and the page number:
Smith 3, at the top right hand corner. Notice that you do not use the word
"page" or its abbreviation. Notice that you do not put your name in all-caps:
SMITH 3. Notice that you do not omit the blank space: Smith3. Notice that you
use numbers, not Roman numerals. Also notice that there is no punctuation,
such as a comma, between the name and page number: Smith, 3. Your name and
page number should be in the top right-hand corner, only one-half inch below
the top of the page and flush with the one-inch right margin. From this, you
double-space down to start your text at the one-inch margin; in other words,
there is only one blank line between the header and the first line of text, not
two. Sometimes, students use their first initial, followed by a period, before
the last name. This is acceptable. The header should look like this:

..............................top of page.........................

                                                              Smith 3
        This would be the first line of your own text. There is only one
        blank line between the header and your text. See? The header is
        one-half inch down, and the first line is a full inch down.

5. How to treat a mistake in a quote.   [sic]

If there is a misspelling in a quotation that you are including, you may insert
[sic] in brackets (do not use parentheses) immediately after the misspelling
to indicate that the misspelling is part of the quotation and not an error
of yours. This word *sic* is the Latin word for THUS and means that you found
the quotation thus--exactly as you see it. Do not overuse [sic] by inserting
it after every idiosyncratic punctuation, British spelling, colloquialism, or
archaic spelling. It will be obvious to the reader that such things are part of
the quotation. You need only insert [sic] when there is a true spelling error
in the quotation. Think of it this way: use [sic] if there is a publisher's
typographical error in the book. If it is not a typo, and the book is printed
the way the publisher wanted it, you do not need [sic].

6. Works Cited title rules.

Construct your Works Cited title correctly. On the Works Cited page, the title
Works Cited should be exactly centered, one inch from the top of the page.
It should not be underlined. It should not be in all-caps, WORKS CITED. It
should not say Work Cited. It should only be double-spaced down from your name
header, not triple or quadruple-spaced, and the works cited should be double-
spaced down from the title. Do not use the outdated term Bibliography because
we now list many works other than books. Please consult the *MLA Handbook* for
guidelines on such matters. The Works Cited title looks like this:

```
............................top of page............................
```

Works Cited

Adamsson, Susan. *Developments in Poetic Forms of the Twentieth Century*.

London: Oxford UP, 1975.

7. Abbreviate publishers in your Works Cited.

Abbreviate publishers' names in the Works Cited listings. In your Works Cited page, you fail to follow the MLA instructions for abbreviating the names of publishing houses. Avoid including unnecessary words such as *Publishing*, *Company*, and *Inc*. Condense long names such as *Harcourt, Brace, Jovanovitch* down into the short ones listed in the *MLA Handbook*: *Harcourt*. Instead of *Charles Scribner's Sons* it is only *Scribner's* (do not forget the apostrophe in that one). *Prentice-Hall* is just *Prentice*. Do not write out the words *University* or *Press*: instead of *Indiana University Press* it is simply *Indiana UP*; instead of *University of Michigan Press* it is simply *U of Michigan P*. Notice that we do not put a period after the *U* or the *P*.

8. Punctuation: ; however,

In a compound sentence in which the second clause begins with a conjunctive adverb such as *however* or *therefore*, use a semicolon between the clauses and a comma after the adverb. For example, you would write, "The author seems sympathetic; however, he is only being ironic."

9. No comma in an ID complex sentence. (ID)

Remember not to use a comma in an ID complex sentence such as "Socrates would not teach because he said he had nothing to teach." If the independent clause comes first, no comma: ID. If the dependent clause comes first, then put a comma: D,I. "Because he had nothing to teach, Socrates would not teach." I expect you to follow the clause punctuation rules we have studied: (I;I I,ccI D,I ID). Every time you write a sentence you must make a conscious clause punctuation decision.

10. First versus firstly.

If you are enumerating elements in your essay, use *first* and *second*, rather than *firstly* and *secondly*. The latter terms with their *-ly* suffixes have a supercilious, pedantic tone to them that is undesirable. In fact Thomas Hardy even satirized the use of such language in one of his poems, "Channel Firing." In the poem, a skeleton wakes up in the grave and muses about someone he knows, "Parson Thirdly."

Discussion Question: Which of the comments would you be most likely to receive on a paper you had written? Which of the comments is the most important? Why?

Academic Thinking: Creating Your Own Idea

As you have seen, we are not writing an elementary-style paper that is only parroting unexamined facts, such as a biographical paper about someone's life, from birth to death, or a list of the facts of tornados. A simple fact report is not appropriate for many reasons, but the most important is that it is intellectually shallow: you can repeat a list of facts without even noticing what the ideas *are*, let alone deciding what you think. At the very least, to write a challenging, meaningful paper, you must rise above the slumber of repeating facts to the realm of ideas. Facts themselves are only a loose pile of construction materials. The point is not just what the facts *are*; it is what you *think* about them, what *you make* of them. Let us review the path we have followed to this point:

1. **Report an idea**. The first level of the idea paper is to report an idea. There is nothing wrong with this. Intellectual history is filled with complex ideas that are worth studying, analyzing, and explaining, and it can be an important accomplishment to do that. In the process, you include facts about the idea itself, the supporting evidence, and perhaps facts about the life of the intellect who created the idea.

2. **Compare and/or contrast ideas**. The second level of the idea paper is to compare and/or contrast more than one idea. This requires you not only to report the facts and ideas but to determine and then report your own observations about similarities and differences among the ideas. Clearly, this is more advanced thinking than simply reporting one idea, but it does not yet require you to assess the truth or validity of the ideas.

3. **Evaluate someone else's idea**. The third level of the idea paper is not only to report the idea or ideas, which is still necessary, but then to assess the truth, using relevant criteria. This can be exceptionally complex, but it moves us deeply into the arena of independent thinking. From this point on, we are not merely reporting or believing what we are told; we are learning to weigh the scholarship and make up our own minds.

4. **Create an idea**. Once we assume a personal, independent identity in the intellectual world, once we begin to decide for ourselves what we think, we realize that sometimes none of the existing ideas, none of the existing interpretations, none of the existing models, is convincing. We ask, which of these ideas is the truth, and the answer is a silent void. That invites us to do better, to create our own term, our own interpretation, our own model. To do so requires us to report the facts, report the ideas, compare and evaluate the ideas, find them still wanting, and then to offer a new solution that solves the problem. This is still done without using the first person pronoun or any other form of self-reference. What does this mean, in more practical terms?

   A single word or short phrase that captures the idea. Theories and concepts are often encapsulated in single words or short phrases. The Bauhaus school of industrial design in the 1920s was called, among other terms, *functionalism*. Let us imagine that you are studying the work of a poet, and several articles describe the poet's poems disparagingly as *technical*—meaning that the poet has good technique but the poems do not mean much. If you think that these critics are missing something, you might develop your own term to contrast with the term *technical*; perhaps you would call the poems *evasive introspection*, or similar words, implying that the poems are deeply but privately self-reflective. You could then use the words *evasive* and *introspection* in your title and in every paragraph as the micro-language to tie the essay together. You would have to find passages in the poems that would illustrate evasive introspection. Notice: you develop your own idea, and then you *give it a name*. It is fun to build up a case like that.

   An elaborate explanation, redefinition, or model. Sometimes our analysis leads us to a more complex picture; we envision the truth in elaborate terms, with one stage leading to another and the second stage leading to a third. We see three things coming together to make a part, and that part affecting another. In these complex situations, we often can create a diagram, with arrows and labels illustrating the points of a process. This can be fun because you get to come up with words to name the parts and words to name the entire system, all of your own design. You might, for example, design a complex explanation to show how various historical factors interact to cause an event.

Proofreading Practice

Keep increasing your estimate of what it takes to do excellent proofreading. Proofreading takes guts; you have to have the steely self-discipline to steer yourself back through the paper, looking at each scrap, even if you are not in the mood. Take a break, then come back and do it again. Make the paper as close to perfect as you can. The more pride you have about not getting caught making elementary errors, the better your paper will be.

Here is the list of elements to check as you proofread the MLA page opposite and its Works Cited page below. How many errors can you find? Notice that every error makes you stop reading; errors interfere with ideas.

- ❏ Grammar
- ❏ Usage
- ❏ Punctuation
- ❏ MLA format
- ❏ Essay structure

- ❏ Connectedness, flow
- ❏ Academic tone
- ❏ Wordiness
- ❏ Word choice

Works Cited   Abbunga, 4

Addy, Mal. *The Courage of Meaning in the Context of Cynicism.* Cambridge: Hampshire UP, 2008.

Camus, Albert. **The Plague.** Chicago: Lakeview, 2004.

---. *The Stranger.* New York: Redoubt, 2002.

Kierkegaard, Soren. *The Concept of Irony, with Constant Refrence to Socrates.* Boston: Trident, 1998.

Surdd, A.B. "Albert Camus: The Misunderstood Icon." *Modren Philosophy and Fiction Quarterly.* 3 (2005): 62-81.

Cal Abbunga

Ms. Pelled

English Honors

21 October 2009

Albert Camus and the Obscurity of Meaning

Ever since the dissident novelist, and philosopher Albert Camus died in 1960, literary critic's have referred to him as an *existentialist*. Camus himself rejected the label, explaining that he was for individualism and against Nihilism. Existentialists attempt to solve the perceived problem of meaningless modern existence--that the modern individual is a lost nonentity without hope--through the individual's intense and authentic exertion of free will, but they often begin with a bleek view of the world, what Surdd has called a "gray and vacuous landscape of objects, void of human meaning" (Surdd 78).

A close examination of Camus's novels *The Stranger* and *The Plague* indicates that Camus--as he claimed--was not an existentialist, that he viewed the world not as without meaning but as meaning-obscured. It may be difficult to define meaning but in Camus's version of the modern world "care continues to exist" (Addy 162), and characters are described with empathy, and identities that matter. At the end of the first chapter of *The Stranger*, an old man express his grief at the protagonist Meursault's mother's funeral:

> His eyes were streaming with tears, of exhaustion or distress, or both together. But because of the wrinkles they couldn't flow down. They spread out, criscrossed, and formed a smooth gloss on the old, worn face (Camus 12).

Visible in Mersault's description is not only the high humanity of the old man, moved to streams of tears at the experience of the mother's funeral, but also the humanity of Meursault, moved--perhaps in spite of himself--by the humanity of the old man's "old worn face." Writing carefully, Camus's description reminds us of the poignant sketches of Leonardo DaVinci. What the description does not convey is a bleakness in which nothing matters. There is meaning. Though it is obscure. We see a

---

Assignment Four • Creating an Idea

The Concept of the Paper

The concept of this paper is to make your own, original contribution to ideas. Higher than reporting, comparing, or even evaluating ideas is creating ideas. This is an extremely advanced level of intellectual work which by its very nature must be regarded as optional (See the caution below). Creating ideas involves all of the three previous levels, but in those three levels we are still working with things we have found. Creating ideas means inventing a new idea and putting it where there was nothing.

A CAUTION: it is not always appropriate or even posssible to do this; often, one of the existing concepts is truly persuasive or the content simply does not lead you to a new term or hypothesis of your own, but this paper will give you an opportunity to think about developing your own ideas. If, after reading and thinking carefully about your research, you cannot arrive at a satisfying idea of your own creation, then you may write a paper discussing an idea or evaluating an idea, but give yourself a chance to enjoy the excitement of putting your own stamp on knowledge if you can.

> **Purpose: Creating a Discipline-Based Idea**
>
> This paper will once again take you below the surface of your course of study, leading you into significant background reading, and causing you to think about the validity of a course-related idea. In the process you will develop your own term, or interpretation, or explanation, or model.

> **Topic: A Discipline-Based Evaluation**
>
> Once again, your teacher will decide which discipline (literature, history, science, or others) this paper will explore. You might be evaluating a literary topic, such as a theme that is attributed to a novelist, or a historical theory about the effect of individuals on society, or a scientific idea. Your teacher may provide you with specific areas of research within the discipline, or you may be given the freedom to choose your own idea from what you find in research; this is the teacher's decision.

Length: Four Pages

This paper must be four pages long with a fifth page for the Works Cited. Page four should contain a half-page or more of text.

Due Date: Provided by Teacher

Your teacher will assign the date, providing at least two weeks for both research and writing. Late papers will lose one letter grade per day.

Format: MLA

This will be an MLA essay with long and short quotations. A paper done in any other format will not be accepted but will be returned to you to be redone. The teacher may assign a letter-grade-per-day penalty for lateness in such a case. The paper should be typed on one side of the page only, in ragged-right, double-spaced Courier type font, ten- or twelve-point size. There must be a minimum of two long quotations and four short quotations in the paper. There is no separate title page.

Structure: Essay

This paper should be a three-part thesis essay, with introduction, body, and conclusion. The paragraphs should be organized and clearly connected. Use a key word from your thesis to connect the paper.

Sources: Five Sources of Fiction and Nonfiction

For this paper you must have a minimum of five sources in your Works Cited page.

Honor: Your Plagiarism Pledge

Before you turn your paper in, you should write on the back of the paper, "I know that plagiarism is the unacknowledged use of someone else's words or ideas, and I pledge that this paper is not plagiarized" and sign it. A plagiarized paper will receive a zero.

Teacher: Your Teacher Is the Authority

For all of these guidelines, your teacher has the final say. If he or she wants to amend any detail, that is final.

Urbarron, 1

Rob Urbarron

Mrs. Ippee

English Honors

4 January 2008

Jane Austen: The Undiscovered Theme

Readers of Jane Austen's most popular novel, *Pride and Prejudice,* have discovered themes of individual pride, class prejudice, and often the assertion of unconventional individuality in a society that demands conformity--particularly of women. In "A Thematic Analysis of Jane Austen's Novels," Mary O'Nette describes Austen's novels as:

. . . a series of miffs, squabbles, and impudent effronteries, a contemptible collection of half-blind, would-be aristocrats who see only their self-perceived social status as their main concern, and a typical portrayal of the British caste behavior in the late 18th century. (O'Nette 172)

Though there are squabbles and effronteries to spare, this standard ...mes fails to discover an underlying theme that may be as ...he disturbing cacophony of

97

Rob,

Your paper is a real contribution, identifying an undiscovered theme in Jane Austen. Certainly, critics have done interpretive work in the general area of your idea, but no one, I think, has captured the essence of this theme so succinctly as you have. Your paper is also well written in standard English, follows the MLA standard strictly, and has excellent essay structure. I like the way you use the word *discover* as your microlanguage to tie the paper together.

Let's look at details to improve when you write the next paper:

Page 3: No comma in an ID complex sentence. (ID)
Remember not to use a comma in an ID complex sentence such as "Socrates would not teach because he said he had nothing to teach." If the independent clause comes first, no comma: ID. If the dependent clause comes first, then put a comma: D,I. "Because he had nothing to teach, Socrates would not teach." I expect you to follow the clause punctuation rules we have studied: (I;I I,ccI D,I ID). Every time you write a sentence you must make a conscious clause punctuation decision.

First versus firstly.

If **you are**

LET YOUR PRINCIPLES BE FEW AND FUNDAMENTAL.

MARCUS AURELIUS
The Meditations

PROOFREAD

- ❏ Grammar
- ❏ Connectedness
- ❏ Usage
- ❏ Academic tone
- ❏ Punctuation
- ❏ Wordiness
- ❏ MLA format
- ❏ Word choice
- ❏ Essay structure

No one's say-so is evidence.

Carl Sagan

If you see an adjective, kill it.

Mark Twain

D,I
ID

I,ccI
I;I

If it is possible to cut out a word, always cut it out.

George Orwell